"*If you yearn for more sacred moments, this book is for you. With a light-hearted approach to a God-filled life, Hanna Perlberger gives you a path to consciously and systematically engage the sacred. Use this year to craft a life of meaning and purpose.*"
- Megan McDonough, CEO and co-founder of Wholebeing Institute

"*A Year of Sacred Moments provides a unique guide to a Torah-based conversation that allows for better clarity, choices, and the way to meaningful and inspired living.*"
- Amy Holtz, Esq., Executive Producer, Crossing the Line 2: The Intifada Comes to Campus

"*For the soul-seeker who is interested in personal and spiritual growth, this innovative and interactive Journal, which interconnects positive psychology coaching with sacred Jewish text, is a must-have!*"
- Dr. Ruth Pinkenson Feldman, Ed.D., author of *The Green Bubbie: Nurturing The Future.*

"*What's unique and so valuable about this book is that it's a guided journal that can engage and accompany readers on their own interactive spiritual journey. And after 54 years of journaling, I can guarantee that it's an effective method for bringing together all the parts of one's self.*"
- Janet Falon, author of *The Jewish Journaling Book*

A Year OF SACRED MOMENTS

THE SOUL SEEKER'S GUIDE TO INSPIRED LIVING

HANNA PERLBERGER

Foreword by Maria Sirois, Psy.D.

BALBOA.
PRESS
A DIVISION OF HAY HOUSE

Balboa Press books may be ordered through booksellers or by contacting:

Balboa Press
A Division of Hay House
1663 Liberty Drive
Bloomington, IN 47403
www.balboapress.com
1 (877) 407-4847

Scriptures taken from The Chumash: Stone Edition. Copyright 1997, 1994 by Mesorah Publications, Ltd., 4401 Second Avenue, Brooklyn, NY 11212, 718 921-9000. Used by Permission

Print information available on the last page.

ISBN: 978-1-5043-8556-5 (sc)
ISBN: 978-1-5043-8558-9 (hc)
ISBN: 978-1-5043-8557-2 (e)

Library of Congress Control Number: 2017912346

Balboa Press rev. date: 10/11/2017

To Bobbie Burdett –

In the end these things matters:
How well did you live?
How fully did you love?
How deeply did you let go?

- Jack Kornfeld

And to my husband Naphtali, and our children

ABOUT THE AUTHOR

Hanna Perlberger is an author, attorney, spiritual teacher, and coach. She speaks to people from all walks of life and helps them in their search for greater happiness, meaning, and spiritual engagement. Hanna and her husband, Naphtali, live in Merion Station, Pennsylvania. For more information, please visit www.ayearofsacredmoments.com.

FOREWORD

In her work, *A Year of Sacred Moments: The Soul Seeker's Guide to Inspired Living*, Hanna Perlberger provides us, fellow seekers, what we both want and what we most need. We want to be made wiser, informed by others who have studied Torah and law and psychology so that we can understand what is important, what is irrelevant and how to brace up when life becomes challenging or confusing.

Hanna has stepped into her full authority here as a student of many disciplines, interweaving knowledge and research from many sources. She creates a breadth and depth of interpretation that provides the novice or long-time seeker with guidance, perspective, and clarity.

At the heart of every seeker is a yearning to know, and with thoughtful, humorous, playful and fierce language, the author answers that longing directly. She also, however, addresses what we most need - whether we are conscious of this need or not. We most need to be held accountable for the application of wisdom into daily living.

We can neither think nor feel our way into a more whole life, a more spiritually fulfilling or healthier life. While knowledge for its own sake is fascinating, when combined with practice, it can be transformative. To reach the life we seek, we must act on our learning. We must choose a daily commitment to shaping our behavior toward that which nourishes us.

With each chapter inviting deep conversation, exploration, and a crafted inquiry to focus attention toward daily application, Hanna Perlberger offers a template for living that is truly inspired, rich, and rampant with meaning.

———————◆—————

Maria Sirois, Psy.D. is an international consultant in the field of Positive Psychology and author of, *A Short Course in Happiness After Loss (and Other Dark, Difficult Times)* and *Every Day Counts: Lessons in Love, Faith and Resilience from Children Facing Illness*. http://www.mariasirois.com/.

INTRODUCTION

For the soul seeker interested in personal and spiritual growth, *A Year of Sacred Moments: The Soul Seeker's Guide to Inspired Living,* provides the means of deep engagement with the sacred - not just for a moment- but to actively and consciously create new behaviors that endure for a lifetime.

Through the blend of the weekly Torah portion, ancient Jewish wisdom and the paradigm of positive psychology and modern thought leaders, each chapter provides the reader with tools and a universally applicable message of personal and spiritual growth. As a workbook, each chapter contains powerful questions and suggested exercises to prompt the reader to discover his or her insights, and with weekly journaling, to record observations, shifts, and experiences. Through journaling, the reader is able to actively process experiences, acquire clarity, and consciously choose new behaviors.

While there is a unique spiritual energy that occurs each week that makes working with the weekly Torah portion especially efficacious, the realm of the sacred is entirely holistic, with each part being a facet of an indivisible whole. And so, the reader may choose to work on a particular theme without regard to the cycle of Torah readings.

A Year of Sacred Moments is designed to illuminate and capture the sacred moments of one's life and become an invaluable companion to narrate the on-going and limitless journey of the soul and illuminate new pathways for inspired living.

ACKNOWLEDGEMENTS

If the act of becoming yourself is a team sport, then I must acknowledge some of my teammates:

To Sara Esther Crispe. One day, Sara Esther approached me to house a writing workshop she was giving on the Ten Commandments, and I instantly agreed. Every week, a small group of women gathered in my living room to read their essays and after I had read one of mine, Sara Esther, who was at the time the editor of The JewishWomen.org, asked if she could publish my piece. *Let me get this straight. You wanna publish what I wrote – and pay me 75 bucks? Heck yes!* Thus, began my creative writing journey. Being a lawyer, I assumed all I could write were briefs, memoranda, and complaints. It was only fitting that as I embarked on this book, Sara Esther was my spiritual midwife. Her editing insights and help in formulating the coaching questions and exercises that gave birth to this book in its final form were invaluable.

To Bobbie Burdett, my Bobbie. For those of you who know me well, you may be surprised at the dedication of this book. Who *is* this woman? Bobbie was one of the pioneers of the wellness movement in the United States and my instructor in holistic wellness coaching. From her, I learned that wellbeing is synonymous with whole being, which is an openhearted inquiry into all of the dimensions of life that make life worth living. Fearlessly curious, she taught me the way of increasing awareness, of being in learner's mind, living the question and not rushing to the safety of problem solving. It's a lot harder than you think. "Build bridges, not walls," she taught, and when faced with challenges, she modeled how to get bigger instead of smaller. Bobbie was the mirror you wanted to look into and the cozy shawl to warm your soul. My holy bro, Will, and I continue to see you in the impossible orange flowers and the synchronized cosmic downloads. Knock 'em alive.

To Laurie Ganger Hubbs. One year the need arose in a local synagogue for a woman speaker to give an address during Rosh Hashanah and unbeknownst to me, my husband volunteered me for the cause. My ensuing panic was so great I thought I would need medical or psychiatric intervention. Instead, I opted to take a speakers workshop with Denise Hedges and Tom Waldenfels. During a magical evening at an inn on the border between North and South Carolina, Laurie drove up and talked me down off the cliff with some pointed questions. "What are you so afraid of?" *"That people will think I'm stupid."* "Well, are you? Are you stupid?" *"Um, I guess not. I mean there's objective evidence that I'm probably not stupid."* Rolling her eyes, she asked, "Do you consider yourself an honest person?" *"Um, yea, I hope so."* "And do you believe in God?" *"Absolutely."* "Then how in the world have you given yourself permission to lie to yourself – and to God – about who you are?" The refusal to admit, much less use our God-given gifts is not humility, but an insult to the Giver. While I tremble at the audacity of even writing such a book as this, *not* writing it is even worse.

To February 13, 2013. My husband suffered a catastrophic medical episode, and his subsequent debilitation and long recovery left me so stressed out and anxious, that he urged me to enroll in the CIPP program (Certificate in Positive Psychology) taught by Tal Ben-Shahar and the gang (Megan McDonough and Maria Sirois and other truly positive people) of the WholeBeing Institute. While the tenets of Judaism resound with teachings of positivity and gratitude, I was not able to access and internalize them at the time. It was, however, through the tools and techniques of Positive Psychology, beginning with keeping a Gratitude Journal, which transformed my negativity into positivity and perceived curses into revealed blessings. Instead of bitterness and disappointment, I was filled with awe at the miracle of my husband's survival under truly dire circumstances. I saw the many kindnesses of my community, family, and friends who made sure my daughter always had a ride to school, my fridge was full, and that we were always in their thoughts and prayers. I came to appreciate that even though this situation did not appear to be for the best, it nevertheless brought out the best in me. My husband's near-death experience happened within a few days of our anniversary. And so, a year later, grateful to be celebrating another anniversary, I started writing weekly blogs (Positive Parsha), which formed the basis of this book, integrating what I was learning from Positive Psychology into the weekly Torah portion. Were it not for the darkness of that night, this book would never have seen the light of day.

To my son, for his read-through of the manuscript, pointing out instances of religious pomposity. To my mother, who posted a comment every week on my blog; I hoped our different last names fooled people into thinking we weren't related. To my many teachers, guides, friends, supporters, readers, soul-sisters and brothers, fellow seekers, strangers in airports and supermarkets, the good and the bad-mannered who wound up as grist for my writing mill, and to the many companions with whom I have and will walk on this path of life, whether for a minute or a mile - I thank you.

As any team has to have a coach, I have to thank my unconditional best friend, my husband, Naphtali, who has been my "yes" man for so many years I have finally begun to believe in the power of that word. If I could see myself through his eyes for a mere five minutes, everything would be possible. And to all of our incredible children, you are the "why" for what I do.

And finally, my gratitude to *HaKodesh Borchu*, the Holy One, Blessed be He, Master and Creator of the universe, who has brought me to this day, and who I believe, is the secret Co-Author of this book.

"Have you ever thought; whilst looking all this time for the magic in the world, it's been inside you all along? No matter how far you travel, how wide you spread your wings and learn to fly, if you have no idea what treasures hide within you you'll be searching your entire life."

- Nikki Rowe

TABLE OF CONTENTS

Book of Bereishit/Book of Genesis

Book of Shemot/Exodus

Book of Vayikra/Leviticus

Book of Bamidbar/Numbers

-BEREISHIT-
GENESIS

WHERE ARE YOU IS A VERY GOOD QUESTION

*(Bereishit/*Genesis 1:1 – 6:8)

> *"Questions are powerful tools. They can ignite hope*
> *and lead to new insights. They can also destroy hope*
> *and keep us stuck in bad assumptions."*

> - Michael Hyatt

In the face of questionable or annoying behavior, we often make the mistake of asking "Why?" For the most part, asking someone "why" questions, such as, "Why are you so disorganized? Why did you leave your wet towel on the floor? Why did you forget to take your lunch to school? Why did you leave on all the lights? Why did you blah blah blah…" are bad questions. How so?

"Why" questions are often less of a genuine inquiry into the truth of the matter and more of a veiled accusation and criticism. When your spouse comes into the kitchen in the middle of the night craving that last bit of beef with broccoli, for example, and finds the empty Chinese food container surreptitiously buried in the trash, there are no really "good" answers to the interrogation that is sure to follow.

Killer Communication

Relationship expert, John Gottman, famously uses the phrase, "The Four Horsemen of the Apocalypse," to refer to the four communication styles that kill relationships, one of which is "Defensiveness." When we feel unjustly accused of something, we defend ourselves by denying, fishing for excuses, blaming, and turning the tables on the accuser to make it his or her fault.[1]

Sometimes, however, we can get triggered, and process an innocent or good question as being a verbal attack – when it isn't. We're all familiar with the story of Adam eating the forbidden fruit and then hiding from God. God never asked Adam *why* he ate the forbidden fruit; God simply asked, "Where are you?"

The Existential Inquiry

Obviously, this wasn't a literal question, with God playing Hide & Go Seek, peering at the bushes and saying, "Come out, come out wherever you are." It was an existential inquiry. "Where are you?" is a probe of the internal mechanism whereby Adam made it OK to disobey God. No matter how destructive the behavior, there is always an inner voice that convinces us that it's OK, justifiable, or even a moral imperative. No one, I dare say, eats chocolate frosted donuts, or is unfaithful to a partner by accident. Multiple choices have to be made and multiple permissions granted for the mind to distort reality and excuse any behavior. God wanted Adam to contemplate the grave consequences of his behavior, because if Adam was hiding from God, and thus, disconnected from his very Creator, where then could he possibly be?

Response - Ability

The antidote for defensiveness is simple - own your stuff. Take responsibility for your part however big or small, in creating the issue. God was hoping that the first man would "man up," learn from his mistake and reconnect. Adam's disobedience, however, had created in him such a deep sense of shame, that he processed God's inquiry as a "why" question; a verbal attack. Consequently, Adam engaged in typical defensive behaviors. Adam blamed his wife for giving him the fruit which he ate, and then he doubled down by blaming God for giving him a wife to begin with.

Even worse, Adam failed to show remorse. The Sages point out that in the Hebrew text, the verb "ate" is in the *future* tense. Incredibly, Adam was in effect admitting that even if he had the chance for a do-over, he would commit the same sin again, that for all time, Adam will eat that apple, because he is not capable of or interested in changing. He's just that apple-eating guy. Having rejected God's overture and bid to repair the relationship, is it any wonder that at that point, God responded, "You're outta here!"

Who Are You?

Rabbi Schneur Zalman of Liadi, (the famous Chassidic rabbi known as the Alter Rebbe)[2] explains that "Where are you?" really means, "Who are you - at this moment of your life?" For as we go through the trials and tribulations of life, as well as its joys and delights, we can imagine that embedded in each situation is God's implied question to us: "Where/who are you now... and now... and here... and here... with this ordeal....or even that triumph?" And ask yourself, "Are you in relationship with God? Are you connected?"

The Hebrew word for "sin" is "cheit." It means, "to miss the mark," and so we are to understand that it is the very nature of transgressions to take us off course. As anyone who uses GPS knows, we often miss a turn, but the first thing that happens when the system re-routes is to pinpoint our location. Unlike the first man, we must be willing to recalibrate our assumptions, to take responsibility for our actions and respond appropriately.

As Viktor E. Frankl, author of "Man's Search for Meaning," said, "Everything can be taken from a man but one thing: the last of the human freedoms - to choose one's attitude in any given set of circumstances, to choose one's own way."[3] "Where are you?" is a very good question. May our answers be good in turn, may our way be clear, and let's not ever be "that guy," unable to come out from behind the bush, hiding from God, bitter at life and who doesn't know where he's going.

Internalize & Actualize:

1. Think about your life right now from an emotional, spiritual and physical perspective. Write down how you would define "where are you" in these three categories. Then, with each one, write down if where you are is where you want to be. If so, why and what can you do to keep it that way? If not, what will you need to change or work on in order to get to where you want to be?

   _____

   _____

   _____

2. *Bereishit* is the very first word in the Torah and begins with the Hebrew letter *"Beit."* *"Beit"* is numerically equivalent to "two" and one of the explanations is a reminder that we are not intended to get through life alone. We all need others with whom to connect, and others need us as well. Think through where you have been versus where you are now (and where you are going), and who in your life has helped you get there. This week, reach out to those people if possible, and let them know how they have helped you.

   _____

   _____

   _____

3. Likewise, we all have people that we feel have gotten in the way of our being able to reach where we want to be. And yet, when we remove our defensiveness, sometimes we find that the very people that created obstacles actually forced us (intentionally or not) to become stronger, more resilient and work that much harder. Think about people or situations to which you have ascribed blame. Imagine removing your defenses, and now write down how they may have helped you - more than you may have wanted to admit.

   _____

   _____

   _____

CRITICISM OR COMPASSION –
WHICH WILL MOVE YOU FORWARD?

*(Noach/*Genesis 6:9 – 11:32)*

*"Awakening self-compassion is often the greatest challenge
people face on the spiritual path."*

- Tara Brach

Here comes Rosh Hashanah again. *This year*, I promise myself, my dreams for my big, actualized and transformed life will come true. *This year*, I will be consistently kind, thoughtful, compassionate, disciplined, etc. So, there's the "me" before the Jewish holidays. And there's the future version of the "me" that I yearn to become.

The Fear of Can I Pull It Off?

And yet, can I pull it off? I seem to stand frozen on the precipice of change. What if I fall flat, come up short, or just never change? After all, my same struggles are still here, and year after year, I seem to be apologizing to the same people (and to God) for the same stuff. For honesty's sake, shouldn't I be more realistic about my future?

Coincidentally, in "*Noach*," I noticed a similar hesitation going on. For an entire year, Noah and his family were cooped up in the Ark. Conditions on the Ark were extremely challenging. It was hot, smelly, dark, and noisy. The animals were a constant burden, not to mention frightening and dangerous. Imagine the emotional trauma of being tossed afloat in raging waters while life, as everyone knew it, was coming to a cataclysmic end.

And now, at long last, the doors of the Ark were flung open. Fresh air! Sunlight! Dry Land! And no one makes a move. No one does the "Happy Dance." Why didn't they have the frenzied urgency of high schoolers on the last day of class? In fact, Noah had to be commanded to order everyone out - and if need be - to force them out against their will! How was this possible?

One of the most common fears we have is the fear of failure, anxious that we won't succeed if we try something new, and that we won't succeed when following our true passions. Our heart shows the way, and yet we stand frozen and afraid to follow.

Look Who's Talkin'

As if on cue, the inner critic takes over as the absolute and unchallenged voice of authority. It urges us not to step out on that dry land. After all, staying on the Ark may be better than facing the challenge of creating civilization anew. And being in that place, stuck between "who you are" and "who you want to be" – where your only real obstacle is yourself – is a painful place. How you deal with that pain makes all the difference of whether you remain trapped or whether you can move forward.

I subscribe to a daily e-mail,[4] and this was today's message: "*One of the most awesome things about liking who you are, approving of yourself, and loving yourself is that you get to hang around with Hanna all day.*" Yea – I know. Trust me; I was rolling my eyes too. And then, as I was about to hit the delete button, I suddenly realized how important this idea is. Honestly, how painful is your day tied to someone you don't like? And that voice - that harsh critical voice - I dare say we would never talk to another person the way we talk to ourselves. This inner conversation keeps us locked in a prison of secret shame and blame, and that is not a place from which we can grow and transform ourselves – or anything or anyone else for that matter.

"Wait," you say, "if I like and approve of myself, or even love myself, then how would I change the things that I need to change? Won't I stay the same? How is that possibly a good thing?" Thanks to shame researcher Brené Brown, we know there is a critical difference between "I *made* a mistake," versus the inner shame that tells us, "I *am* a mistake."[5] See the distinction? We can love ourselves even when we blunder. Acknowledging mistakes lets us figure out a better way. Shame, on the other hand, keeps us stuck in what doesn't work. Try as we may, we can't hate our way to spiritual growth or solutions.

The Methodology of Loving Self-Talk

So, what do we do with that fear that keeps us in the Ark? How do we engage the voice that lies in wait for us to mess up again to prove we will never change and that it's folly to bother? Here's one strategy that I suggest - **C.A.R.E.** – which I learned from positive psychology coach, Lynda Wallace:[6]

Catch. Notice when you're engaging in punishing self-criticism. Observe how the inner critic uses a minor slip-up to try to get you to give up completely, convincing you that you will never obtain your goals.

Acknowledge: Recognize the pain that the self-criticism is causing. Find the emotion in your heart and your body. Don't resist it, just allow it and send it compassion.

Request: Speak gently to your self-critic: (*I know you're trying to help, but you're not actually helping, and you are causing me unnecessary pain. Please stop being so self-critical.*)

Encourage: Replace the critical self-talk with supportive self-talk, such as a wise and caring friend might offer. How would you speak to a friend who was down on herself? Give yourself the gift that you freely give others – an understanding and compassionate heart that speaks truthfully, but with kindness and empathy.

In my list of goals to accomplish in anticipation of the New Year, self-compassion was not even on my radar. As I stand now, however, wanting to take a step out of my comfort zone, I understand that treating my fear with contempt and harsh self-evaluation will only guarantee that I remain in place.

Ironic as it may seem, it is through self-compassion, liking ourselves, and yes – even loving ourselves - that we can move forward. Self-compassion is the emotional stance that reveals potential. And it is self-compassion that permits us to converge the "who we are" with the "who we want to be." Self-compassion lets us spend the days of our lives hanging out in the company of someone we kinda like. And then, anything is possible.

Internalize & Actualize:

1. Sit in a quiet room, close your eyes and say out loud: *"You deserve self-compassion. You deserve kindness. You are worthy of goodness."* Now write down the first thoughts that come to your mind. How does saying this make you feel?

    _____

    _____

    _____

2. Now focus on your inner critic. Think about something you are hesitant to do or try because you fear you won't succeed. What messages is your inner critic giving you? Make a short list of all the things you would do if that inner critic were dismissed altogether.

    _____

    _____

    _____

3. Look at that list of what you would ideally do if the inner critic weren't talking to you. Now, in very practical ways, write down five things you can begin to do immediately to work towards these goals. It could be as simple as making a phone call or researching options online, but make that list so that by next week you can know that you have put the inner critic aside and started working in the direction you need to go.

    _____

    _____

    _____

THE JOURNEY OF THE LIMITLESS SELF

(*Lech Lecha*/Genesis 12:1 – 17:27)

"What God intended for you goes far beyond anything you can imagine."

- Oprah Winfrey

For anyone who enthusiastically embraces change, the well-known Biblical directive to Abraham, "Go for yourself from your land, from your relatives, and from your father's house to the land that I will show you"[7] embodies the paradigm of transformation.

Note the peculiar sequence, however, when God commanded Abraham to go from his "country," his "place of birth" and finally, his "father's house." Many point out that since Abraham was traveling by foot, the word order be in reverse. After all, logistically, he would have to leave his home, and then his city and then finally cross the border of his country. Another common question is why did God tell Abraham the places he must leave rather than give clear instructions where he is to go?

The Sequence of Change

When we want to change and break out of a pattern, some ways of being and thinking are more ingrained than others. Therefore, the word order here is reversed for a reason. Abraham's mission was not just physical but spiritual, and so the construct reflects a growing spiritual challenge. Like peeling an onion, "*Lech Lecha*" removes the core set of influences that shape us by starting with what is external and psychologically easiest and then going deeper and deeper.

Our "country" refers to how we are influenced and biased by our contemporary society, our culture, the times, etc. Our "birthplace," on the other hand, refers to our nature, our inherited genes, and our dispositions. *I am a born worrier. That's just who I am.* Our "father's house," which is perhaps the most influential of all, refers to our childhood, and the nurture – or lack thereof - that we received…and it goes deeper. *My father abandoned me as a child, and now I will never allow myself to be vulnerable and trust another man again.* Usually, it is from these unchallenged beliefs that our most limiting and self-sabotaging behaviors come.

In forging a new spiritual path, both Abraham and Sarah needed to go beyond the excuses many of us make for ourselves for why we can't change or grow. "*Lech Lecha*" is not about leaving a geographical location as much as it is about shedding limitations. If we remain trapped as a victim of our circumstances (nature, nurture, and society) then what are we doing with our lives? Either we stay stuck, or we break free; we are either a casualty or an adventurous survivor. Says Rabbi Daniel Levitt:

> Without proper introspection in order to identify the factors that influence the way we act and make decisions, then we just float through life without truly acting out of free will. God is telling Avraham, that sometimes, in order to have a spiritual awakening we have to remove ourselves from the influence of external factors.[8]

The Inner Journey

By emphasizing the process of *leaving* rather than the *arriving,* God is emphasizing that the journey is just as important (and in some cases, more so) than the destination. After all, the literal translation of "*Lech Lecha*" means to "go for yourself" or to "go *to* yourself." Properly understood, all journeys are inner journeys. It's a common theme that sometimes we have to leave what is familiar and known to find our inner qualities. As we grow, we are faced with new challenges. We never really "get there." In fact, there is no such place as "there." But that's the very point. You never completely arrive.

One Small Letter, One Giant Leap

Before their journey, Abraham and Sarah were Abram and Sarai. In *Lech Lecha,* however, one letter transformed each of their names. The insertion of the Hebrew letter *"hei"* changed Abram to Abraham. And by changing the last letter of her name to a *"hei,"* Sarai became Sarah.

The letter *"hei"* is one the letters of the Tetragrammaton, the four-letter name of God's name (YHVH). The sound of the letter *"hei"* is like a breath, alluding to the fact that God breathed life into Adam. Similarly, the spiritual infusion attained by their new names gave Abraham and Sarah a higher level of holiness and sacred purpose. Thus, the journey that they set out on had profound implications not just for them, but also for future generations, as they became prototypes of what was possible in the relationship between man and God.[9]

Their names weren't changed, however, until they had already set out on their journey. Permanent change of one's essence only follows the leap of faith and the transition that must first occur. Avram and Sarai set out on what they were to accomplish, and as they began to actualize their potential, they received their new names - for they were no longer the people they had been previously. Positive change changes who we are.

You Are Still You

Breaking free of limitations, however, doesn't mean that we give up our personal history, or that we instantly morph into someone entirely new. In becoming conscious choosers, therefore, we expand into better versions of ourselves. We peel those layers of constriction to uncover what is truer, deeper, more authentic, congruent and integral. It's a hard fact that we can't shortchange the process, and therefore the inner journey of self-discovery is necessarily one step at a time. But take a deep breath and take heart - you only need one small letter to start.

Internalize & Actualize:

1. Jot down three areas you want to improve. It could be specific or more amorphous, such as you want to lose 10lbs, or you want to be happier. Why are these goals important to you? How do you think your life will change when you reach these goals?

   _____

   _____

   _____

2. Then, write down one *practical* thing that you can do, immediately, to start working towards each of these goals, (e.g., I will start walking 30 minutes two times a week, I will set aside 30 minutes to call a close friend or family member who I love and miss, etc.). Make sure that what you commit to is doable with your schedule and lifestyle.

   _____

   _____

   _____

3. Over the next few weeks come back to this page and write down how the process is making you feel. As discussed, the journey is as important (if not more so) than the actual goal. What are you learning along the way? What is the process teaching you about yourself? Make sure to date each entry so you can see your progress in writing.

   _____

   _____

   _____

THE UNBINDING OF OUR CHILDREN

(*Vayeira*/Genesis 18:1 – 22:24)

Children aren't ours to possess or own in any way.
When we know this in the depths of our soul,
we tailor our raising of them to their needs, rather
than molding them to fit our needs.

- Shefali Tsabary

My husband attended the wedding of a Jewish client of ours, and he came home shaking his head in disbelief at what her rabbi said during the ceremony. "I bless you both that you *never* become like Abraham. Abraham had faith so blind that he was willing to sacrifice his son, Isaac because God told him to. May you never be so blindly obedient."

While I thought that was an inappropriate and controversial thing to say to a couple under a marriage canopy, a lot of people have trouble with the story of the "Binding of Isaac." It's easy to get morally confused and outraged, not just at Abraham for obeying, but also at God for commanding such a thing. Would you kill your kids if God told you to?" (Parents of teenagers need not answer that question.) And even if it was all just a "test," what kind of God puts a parent through a test like that? Either way you slice it, the story of the "Binding of Isaac" can be troubling, and sadly, can incur disdain for its so-called "blind followers."

How do we modern parents fare with this dilemma? For those of us who are unsettled by this story, I have a question: "What is our excuse for sacrificing our children - when we are not acting under God's command?"

The Unconscious Parent

OK, calm down. We are all guilty of this in some way or other. At some point, we all trample our children's sensitivities when we refuse to see their individuality and we find their process of individuation threatening. At times, we are blind to their best qualities while we magnify what we perceive as their faults. Occasionally, we even throw them under the bus so long as they further our agendas or made us look good (for their sake, of course). And if that's not sacrificing a child, I don't know what is.

We all have basic needs, but at certain stages of our lives, some needs are more prominent that others. Common to all humans is the need for love and connection; it's hard-wired into us. For teens, however, it is of particular importance. When children do not necessarily fit the mold of their environment, the message they receive is that unless they conform, they have no value, no worth and no place at the table. Those children have few ways to find that sense of belonging they so desperately crave.

Some kids buckle and try to appear outwardly conforming while being internally conflicted and filled with shame stemming from their lack of authenticity and congruence. Other children look for a peer group or community that welcomes them, and that sends the message – "You're fine as you are. After all, you are just like us."

While parents prefer the external guise of conformity, it is the latter that is better for a child's psyche, unless, of course, the child falls in with people who are very dysfunctional and self-destructive. Unfortunately, however, feelings of rejection make that a very common scenario. When that happens, many parents disconnect from their child, creating a negative downward spiral. Those parents, who realize that children have their unique souls and journeys can be spared from that unfortunate dynamic. While it may not have soothed his pain, nevertheless, an important aspect of Abraham's test was whether he recognized that Isaac belonged not to him - but to God.

In her book, *The Conscious Parent*, Shefali Tsabary, explains: "When you parent, it's crucial you realize you aren't raising a 'mini-me,' but a spirit throbbing with its own signature. For this reason, it's important to separate who you are from whom each of your children is."[10]

Parents can be emotionally abusive when they feel denied the vicarious satisfaction of living their dreams through their children. "You could have been a doctor!" is no joke when parents look at and treat their children as failures for not pursuing their own imaginary dreams. It goes even beyond a proprietary interest when parents can't distinguish children's journeys from the paths they never took. Other parents hypocritically expect their children to be perfect in the areas where they are deficient. When the child fails to measure up, either mirroring the parents' faults or not providing cover for their inadequacies, the reactions can be cruel.

The Gift of Transformation

On a lesser note, parents and children simply have different needs and different wants. Despite the challenge, parents need to handle this clash of needs with sensitivity. Unquestionably, there are plenty of situations where the wishes of the parents will override the desires of the child. However, when it comes to our children discovering and developing who they are, that is when we need to take a step back and ensure that our focus is what is best for them, and not what is best for us.

Niels Bohr, the Nobel Prize winner in physics, said, "The opposite of a true statement is a false statement, but the opposite of a profound truth can be another profound truth." And so it is with the Binding of Isaac. On one hand, it is true that we don't have kids to meet our needs; we have them to meet theirs. But it is also profoundly true, on the other, that the children that we are given are the very children through whom *we* can learn the deepest lessons we need for *our* transformation.

And so, I hope that you do indeed follow in the footsteps of Abraham. And, in so doing, I ask you to ponder what you could give up and lay upon the altar, so as to transform your inner self and, in so doing, become a better and more conscious parent?

Internalize & Actualize:

1. Think about someone whose choices differ greatly from yours where you find yourself in constant disagreement with this person and where you find yourself trying to persuade him or her to adopt your perspective. (This doesn't have to be a child – it could be your spouse or another family member, or a co-worker, etc.)

   _____

   _____

   _____

2. Now write down three ways that you can let go of what you want and help support this person in what is important to him or her, without compromising on your values or beliefs.

   Three ways:

   _____

   _____

   _____

3. Think about how you hope this shift in your behavior towards this person will help improve your relationship. Now write down what goals you hope to accomplish, and then, during this week, implement those three ways listed above and then jot down how it was received and how it made you feel.

   Goals:

   _____

   _____

   _____

   What happened and how it made you feel:

   _____

   _____

   _____

WEAVING THE GARMENTS
OF OUR LIVES

(*Chayei Sarah*/Genesis 23:1 – 25:18)

"When you waste a moment, you have killed it in a sense, squandering an irreplaceable opportunity. But when you use the moment properly, filling it with purpose and productivity, it lives on forever."

- the Lubavitcher Rebbe

Many years ago, a product came on the market called "Death Insurance." The problem was that no one wanted to buy a "death insurance" policy. It was a huge flop – until someone had the bright idea to change the name from "Death Insurance" to "Life Insurance," a much happier and more optimistic name (even though it was the same thing). That little change turned that product from a dud into a gazillion-dollar business.

Chayei Sarah begins with the death of our matriarch, Sarah. "*Chayei Sarah*," literally means, "the Life of Sarah." So, is this a switcheroo, a mere marketing gimmick to uplift us, or is it one of those paradoxical teaching moments?

The Talmud explains how those who are righteous, who fill their days in productive and positive ways, are considered alive when they are dead, while those who bring toxicity and negativity into this world are viewed as dead even while they are alive. And so, it is quite fitting, that following the death of Sarah, we focus on the meaning and influence of her life, who she was and what she accomplished, even though she is no longer living.

Sarah died at the age of 127, and rather than simply tell us that Sarah was 127 years old when she passed away, the Torah curiously describes her lifespan in a curious way: "Sarah's lifetime was one hundred years, twenty years, and seven years."[11] And so, a year is not a year. (Just think how two hours engrossed in watching a riveting show feels compared to two hours sitting through a boring lecture. In one case, time flies, whereas in the other, time stands still.) Time is relative. It is defined more by its quality than its quantity. Sarah's life was filled with many days of challenges and hardships, and yet each day was fully lived as an opportunity to make meaningful and moral choices.

Choosing Ultimate Reality

There is a mystical idea that our days on earth will ultimately comprise the garments that clothe our soul after we die. These garments are those of "thought," "speech" and "action." The quality of these garments will not be determined by the "years of our life," but by the "life in our years." In other words, we stitch together these holy garments from our good deeds, (our *mitzvot*), and the moments we create that we endow with the quality of ultimate meaning, and therefore, infinite reality. For example, someone could live to a ripe old age, and yet, sadly, have lived a life of such little significance and substance, that his or her soul could be naked or virtually naked in the next world. As Eleanor Roosevelt said: "One's philosophy is not best expressed in words; it is expressed in the choices one makes. In the long run, we shape our lives, and we shape ourselves. The process never ends until we die. And the choices we make are ultimately our own responsibility."

Each day of our lives presents us with endless possibilities. We constantly stand at the crossroads of choice. How many times have I thought, "Sorry God, I have no time to pray. I am just so darn busy. Catch you later. Maybe tomorrow?" Thinking I am choosing "reality," you know, "getting stuff done," I fritter away many moments of time that at the end of the day, evaporate like smoke. It's like consuming empty calorie junk food instead of nutrient-rich food filled with vitality. I think I am eating, but, nutritionally, I'm not. It's OK once in a while, but I certainly wouldn't make a habit of it.

When we consciously embrace our lives moment-by-moment, cognizant of the power and significance of our choices, mindfully aware of our words and deeds, we can weave together holy garments that will wrap us like a hallowed shawl.

Close Versus Connected

The Hebrew word for sacrifice, namely the sacrifices that were brought to the Holy Temple, is "*korban*." The root of that word is "*makarev*" which means "to bring/come close." Hence, we are to understand that the purpose of bringing a sacrifice is to come closer to God, and we have opportunities every single moment, to actively move towards where we want to be.

The holiest offering which was brought into the Temple, however, was the "*ketoret*," the incense offering. The word itself means "to bond" or "to connect." It represents the weaving together of different elements to form one unified entity that does not come undone. It is here that I recognize how I am inextricably linked and interconnected with God. While I do my part by "coming close" in my "thought," "speech" and "action," my soul is already there and bonded.

Leveraging Time

And in so doing - since the soul does not die - it's as if we don't truly die. Sarah physically died. That's the truth. But the opposite was also true. As a woman whose life was alive with the fullness of her choices, Sarah also lived, as death only marked a new form of her life. Sarah embodies the idea that we must not merely count our days, but we must make our days count.

So, make the most of every moment. Make your moments holy. Make your moments endure by weaving them into a sacred reality. By understanding the infinite power and potential of each moment, you can stitch together the fabric of your life so that your spiritual loveliness will be there to embrace and clothe your eternal soul. As Jonathan Swift said, "May you live all the days of your life." Happy weaving!

Internalize & Actualize:

1. Starting with the moment you wake up, list four small things you can incorporate into your day to infuse it with meaning and holiness. Think of something to do morning, afternoon, evening and before bed. This could be a few minutes of meditation upon arising, giving gratitude for the food you are eating for breakfast, dedicated focus about those you love in your life, appreciation that you have a roof over your head, etc. The goal is to stop, think and actively acknowledge these things:

   Four actions:

   _____

   _____

   _____

2. Write down something you struggle with and with which you have a hard time being positive. It can be physical or spiritual. Then, tapping into the garments of your soul, commit to shifting your thought, speech and action about that struggle in a practical way on a daily basis. Write down a small step you can take and then make sure to think it, say it out loud and do something towards being positive.

   _____

   _____

   _____

   Struggle:

   _____

   _____

   _____

   Thought, Speech, Action:

   _____

   _____

   _____

HEROIC HUMILITY – AN UNCOMMON VIRTUE

(Toldot/Genesis 25:19 – 28:9)*

"The quieter you become, the more you can hear."

- Anonymous

An American humorist once quipped, "There are two kinds of people in the world. Those who believe there are two kinds of people in the world and those who don't." In the 1920's, Carl Jung introduced the theory, reinforced by personality tests today, that the two kinds of people that exist in the world are either "introverts" or "extroverts."

Introversion and Extroversion in the Torah

This concept is nothing new, as these personality categories are the very archetypes of our forefathers, Abraham and Isaac. Abraham, the prototypical extrovert, is associated with the characteristic of *"chesed,"* which means "kindness." As the father of outreach, Abraham's kindness manifested as an outward expression of love and benevolence to humanity. On the other side of the scale is his son Isaac, the prototypical introvert, to whom is attributed *"gevurah,"* meaning "strength," and who is described as being inner-directed, reserved, and self-disciplined, even to a fault.

As any child of a super charismatic parent knows, growing up in the shadows is hard. Part of that is due to our worship of the extrovert. As Susan Cain, author of the book, *Quiet: The Power of an Introvert in a World That Can't Stop Talking*, notes: "A widely held, but rarely articulated belief in our society is that the ideal self is bold, alpha, and gregarious. Introversion is viewed somewhere between disappointment and pathology."[12]

Accordingly, following in a super parent's larger-than-life footsteps is almost impossible. How many times does an innovative and groundbreaking venture fail, because the next generation is unable to keep the vision alive? And yet, it is Isaac, ostensibly the first "nerd" in Jewish history, who in fact held it all together, and who was responsible for transmitting and promulgating Judaism to the next generation.

The Legacy of Isaac

In the few stories we know about Isaac, he was never the driver of the story. The only narrative where Isaac was the main active protagonist was in connection with Abraham. After Abraham died, the Philistines stopped up the wells Abraham had dug. Here, we read the story of Isaac digging up those old wells, and when the Philistines filled them in again, Isaac re-dug them yet another time, until he ultimately prevailed. Like that's a big deal? Actually, yes, it is.

"*Toldot*," which means "generations," starts out with the words: "These are the generations of Isaac."[13] And yet, the very next sentence is not about Isaac's children, but about Isaac's father, Abraham. Typically, *toldot* refers to progeny; sometimes, however, it means one's legacy. In this case, the Torah directs us to look backward to understand the import of Isaac's lasting legacy.

When to Cultivate and When to Integrate

Rabbi David Fohrman, a popular commentator on Torah topics writes:

> Isaac is about picking up the torch, about consolidating Abraham's legacy, about re-digging the wells to keep his father's vision alive one more generation. If he can do that, the vision is real, it has roots; it will survive. Sometimes your job in life is to innovate, sometimes your job in life is to consolidate. Consolidating isn't as flashy as innovating; it takes great humility to focus your life on striking roots for a great idea that has been innovated by someone else. But that humility is heroic, and that perhaps was the legacy of Isaac.[14]

In a society immersed in individualism, focused on the self and permeated with idealizing the extrovert, we would do well at times to emulate Isaac's humility and value the quiet hero. When we dig wells, we turn inward to reveal that which is hidden. When we tap into our deepest meaning, our inner strengths, and significant values, we can create the type of legacy that we would want to survive us.

Internalize & Actualize:

1. Building a well is the act of digging deep in the earth to ultimately find and expose the wellsprings within. Write down five positive aspects of yourself that are not readily noticeable but that one would find if they dug deep enough.

   _____

   _____

   _____

2. Would you like these parts of you to be more on the surface? If not, why do you keep them hidden? And if so, how you can try to incorporate these qualities into what is most external about yourself?

_____

_____

_____

3. Do you consider yourself an introvert or an extrovert? Or a combination of both? As both personality types have very positive attributes, what can you find in the other personality type that you can work on bringing into your more natural personality type? How do you think this will help round you out?

_____

_____

_____

AN ATTITUDE OF GRATITUDE

(*Vayeitzei*/Genesis 28:10 – 32:3)

When it comes to life the critical thing is whether you take things for granted or take them with gratitude.

- Gilbert K. Chesterson

Here's a Trivial Pursuit question for you - which is anything but trivial: Who was the first person ever to say "Thank You" to God? OK, I'll give you a hint – the answer is in "*Vayeitze*i." And the correct response (which hardly anyone gets right, by the way) is…our Matriarch Leah. Leah was the first person - in recorded history - to express gratitude to God, and she did so when she gave birth to her fourth son, naming him Yehuda, from the word, "*hoda'ah*," which means, "to thank."

Now, this raises a pretty big question. Why didn't Leah say "thank you" when her first child was born? Or her second, or, her third, for that matter? How was it that she waited until her fourth to officially thank God for this baby?

At a quick glance, we are taught that Leah understood that her husband, Jacob, was destined to have 12 sons. Jacob had four wives, and so Leah did the math. When she gave birth to her third son, it seemed that she had been given "her share" which would have been the case if the 12 sons were divided equally amongst the wives. But this fourth child was a genuine surprise. He was unexpected. Therefore, she was overwhelmed with gratitude for this extra share over and above what she had perceived to be her lot.

But does this then mean that Leah was not grateful for her first three children? Not at all! Leah faced a lot of challenges and was filled with insecurities within her marriage and her role in her family. Yet, she was simultaneously self-aware and communicated her needs to God, and with each child, she felt blessed that this baby was the fulfillment of her prayers.

When she birthed her fourth son, however, Leah recognized that she had been purely gifted. It was not just that she had prayed, and her prayers had been answered; but that God had provided Leah with the greatest blessing that she hadn't even requested! This is the child that then received the name "Yehuda" for pure, unadulterated thanks. More so it is the reminder to us that we never fully understand (or sometimes we never understand at all) our situations and circumstances. But when we are grateful for what we have, then we find the meaning and purpose in who we are and what we are capable of.

This is why the Jewish people have been called by many names, but in the end, we are always "*Yehudim*," "Jews," related to the name "Yehuda." Judaism (Yehuda-ism) therefore, can be understood as the means by which we can most fully express what we are at our core – beings who are grateful to God and who show that appreciation.

Ingratitude 101

Unfortunately, it seems that society has become more and more self-consumed, and one of the first things to go is the attitude of gratitude. This approach is a breeding ground for unhappiness. One of the ways we generate dissatisfaction is taking goodness for granted and focusing on what we don't have instead of what we do have. When we take goodness for granted and feel that we are entitled to the good in our life, why should we be grateful? After all, it's "what's coming to me." If we feel that we "deserve it," then it's not a "gift." Therefore, we can't see it as a blessing. Conversely, if we are not getting what we believe to be our "fair share," then we will be pretty unhappy. And we certainly can't feel a sense of thanks when we are coming from a mindset of "lack."

The Pain of Comparisons

In her book, *Self-Compassion*, Kristin Neff describes a woman who emerged from her annual work review floating on air.[15] Her boss said he was so pleased with her performance that she was getting a 10% pay raise. She immediately called her boyfriend to share the good news and, being elated for her, he promised her a champagne celebration when she came home.

As she was leaving work, however, she happened to overhear a coworker talking on her cell phone to a friend. "Can you believe it?" she said, "My boss was so impressed with me that he gave me a 15% pay raise – 5% more than the automatic 10% that everyone else got!"

When she heard that news, the 10% increase was no longer a cause for elation for her; rather, it only created resentment, discontent, and shame that she was not worthy of more. Since the 10% pay raise was what she was entitled to – and no more – she could no longer see it as a source of blessing for which she should be grateful. Thus, a sense of entitlement kills gratitude.

It helps to remember that many people are far less fortunate than you are – and are quite happy with what they have. I saw a sign on a dorm wall that said: "**What if you woke up today only with the things that you thanked God for yesterday?**"

When we understand that everything is a gift, we escape the trap of an entitlement mentality. And when we develop an "Attitude of Gratitude" then we can see and appreciate all of our many blessings. In the words of Melody Beattie: "Gratitude unlocks the fullness of life. It turns what we have into enough, and more. It turns denial into acceptance, chaos to order, confusion to clarity. It can turn a meal into a feast, a house into a home, a stranger into a friend."

Internalize & Actualize:

1. Often we find it easy to be grateful when things are going our way, and are resentful when they are not. Think about five things that are currently not the way you want them to be. Write them down. Now, underneath that list, write down something that you can be grateful for and that is specifically related to the item

above. For example: "I am overweight" (negative). "I am blessed to have plenty of food and have never gone hungry" (gratitude). Or: "I have a terrible relationship with my mother-in-law" (negative). "My children are blessed to have a grandmother in their lives and my husband to have his mother in good health" (gratitude).

Five things you wish were different:

_____

_____

_____

Five things connected to these things you can be grateful for:

_____

_____

_____

2.   Think about three things you feel entitled to in your life that other people would consider blessings (i.e., I deserve a vacation for how hard I work…). Now write down three ways you can immediately begin to express gratitude for those things or areas of your life.

Three areas of entitlement:

_____

_____

_____

Three ways to express gratitude:

_____

_____

_____

3.   There are so many things in our lives that we don't even recognize as blessings because they are considered "normal." Think about how many times we complain about a "boring" day, rather than being grateful that nothing terrible happened.

This week, every night before you go to sleep, think through your day and jot down everything there is to be grateful for that you often take for granted (i.e., I woke up, kids are healthy, I have my job, I got to work on time, I finished my project, etc.) You specifically want to focus on the ordinary and each day make sure you write down some different things on your list. Each day that you make your list write how it makes you feel to focus on these areas and to consider them blessings.

Gratitude Journal: Week 1

_____

_____

_____

How does it make you feel?

_____

_____

_____

NO BAD ANGELS – HOW TO ENGAGE CREATIVELY WITH STRESS

*(Vayishlach/*Genesis 32:4 – 36:43)*

The heart must face its tests.
Only then can we discover who we really are
and what extraordinary things we are capable of achieving.

- James O'Dea

No one gets through life without being tested, repeatedly. So, when we come face to face with the terrors that can keep us up at night, how do we achieve grace under fire? *"Vayishlach"* contains the famous episode of Jacob wrestling with the angel. At long last, brother Esau is ready to exact revenge for the "stolen" birthright and has come with a small army to confront Jacob. In advance of that confrontation, Esau sent his "angel" to do battle with Jacob to weaken him before their encounter.

However, Jacob was no stranger to this dynamic. Clashing with Esau in the womb, Jacob's earliest encounter with conflict began in utero. Born in the midst of a power struggle, Jacob lived a life that can be characterized as one challenging battle after another - more or less what we would call "the human condition." But is that such a bad thing?

The Disempowered Reaction to Stress

Some people engage stress by reacting in these opposite ways: they becoming super aggressive and even violent, *or* they abruptly disconnect. Others, however, take the middle road of passivity, where they try to avoid any form of conflict, even at a cost to their well-being, vested interests or personal integrity. People who are frightened of conflict will cling to being "non-confrontational" to avoid difficult individuals or situations.

If you asked such people whether conflict avoidance works as an effective strategy, however, the honest ones would admit that it does not. Whether they become entirely passive or passive-aggressive, these folks are simply trading one form of suffering for another.

Similarly, have you ever noticed that the very people who complain so bitterly about wanting to be "free from suffering" seem so unbelievably attached to it? They insist that stress is an external and arbitrary imposition that keeps them from being happy – which is just so unfair! Offer them a solution, a new mindset, or a coping strategy, however, and they are not so quick to get on board. Oddly, we seem addicted to the very thing we say we don't want.

Never Letting a Crisis Go to Waste

In "*Vayishlach*," Jacob gives us a role model that takes the engagement with conflict to a new level of empowerment and transformation. In his previous conflict with Esau, Jacob was not "straight" with his brother. (While it was pre-destined that Jacob would receive the first-born blessing, there is still much discussion amongst the Torah commentators criticizing *how* he went about getting it.) When it came to obtaining the blessings for the first-born, Jacob did an end-run around his brother, which caused Jacob to have to flee for his life. Twenty years later, Jacob came *towards* his brother. In taking his family away from the household of his father-in-law, Jacob could have circumvented him again and avoided him entirely. This time, however, Jacob sent messengers to let Esau know he was coming. And in so doing, he set the stage for the encounter, because at last, he was playing it straight.

It wasn't merely that Jacob didn't avoid the conflict. Rather, he didn't waste his time and energy with resentment and complaint. Instead, Jacob prepared himself to engage. While the text is translated as "prepared," the term literally means, "repaired." Thus, when Jacob centered himself with truth and integrity, he repaired himself.

And so, when this transformed version of Jacob wrestled with Esau's angel, Jacob authentically engaged the angel "full-out," while at the same time, remaining humble. And then, at the end of the nightlong struggle, when Jacob prevailed, he did something that seems to make no sense. Jacob asked the angel to reveal its name and to give him a blessing. Imagine getting mugged, and then asking the mugger for a blessing. So, what could we learn from such a strange request?

Consider this – if we confront a stressor with a direct encounter - face it, engage it, and wrestle with it – then we can learn from it and even make it our teacher. It is then that it can become a source of blessing. Relationship experts, Harville Hendrix and Helen LaKelly Hunt, like to reframe conflict as "growth trying to happen."[16] And as Viktor E. Frankl, said, "Suffering ceases to be suffering at the moment it finds a meaning."[17]

And so, stress will either open you up or shut you down. Those are the only two possibilities. If you choose to open up, you may stay engaged with the discomfort, but by wrestling with its meaning, you will see that there are lessons to be learned and that the pain can help free you to become a bigger, better and wiser human being. Like Jacob, you too can emerge from the darkness of fighting with your stress and challenges into the dawn of a new persona. Is that not a blessing?

Internalize & Actualize:

1. What stressful situation or person in your life have you been coping with through aggression, denial, blame, stonewalling, or disproportionate attack? Write down the feelings that arise when you think about the situation or person. Next to each feeling, write if it is a positive feeling that promotes growth or a negative one that causes stagnation.

   Stressful situation/person:

   _____

   _____

   _____

Feelings about this situation/person. Positive or Negative?

_____

_____

_____

2. Now, reflecting on what you just wrote, make this situation (not the person but rather what that person represents) your "teacher." Think about ways you can learn from it (even if your lesson is to do just the opposite, for knowing what *not* to do is a gift). List five possible positive outcomes from what until now you saw as purely negative.

    Five positive outcomes:

    _____

    _____

    _____

3. We often try to avoid stress and stressful situations whenever possible. Think through some things or people you have been intentionally avoiding. Then think about proactive ways you can engage and deal with them by choice rather than waiting until it is unavoidable. Write down today's date and commit to doing one thing this week to work towards a practical action you can take to address this. Then, after a week, write down if you feel any differently about it through purposely engaging something you previously avoided.

    Date /Situation /One Practical Action:

    _____

    _____

    _____

    Follow up Date/Reflections:

    _____

    _____

    _____

AND SUDDENLY...IT ALL MADE SENSE

(*Vayeishev*/Genesis 37:1 – 40:23)

*"Optimist: Someone who isn't sure whether life is a tragedy
or a comedy but is tickled silly just to be in the play."*

–Robert Brault

The Search for Understanding

I was walking down the main thoroughfare in my neighborhood – my very staid suburban neighborhood – when I became aware of someone behind me. I half turned around to see a man on a bicycle coming up slowly on my right, so slowly that we were able to make eye contact and a quick, friendly nod as he pedaled past me.

And as he biked ahead of me, my brain performed an automatic scan. *Man on bike.* Check. *Wearing cool black and yellow spandex biking gear.* Check. *Wearing a helmet.* Check. *Wearing a big video camera mounted on his helmet.* Huh? And....what...am....I....looking...at? The next incoming phrase *and he's wearing a pink effervescent tutu*, was so bizarre and out of context that my brain had trouble putting the words to what my eyes were in fact, seeing.

It's not like I never saw a guy in a pink tutu before; a man by the name of "Rollerina" used to roller-skate at high speed in the streets of New York

City, where I lived in the late 1970's. But it's out of character for where I reside now, and it didn't jive because nothing else about the bicyclist was unusual. Except for maybe the camera thing – and what was that about?

A few more steps and I noticed a small black sign stuck into the ground on my right. The white letters read: "Early detection makes the best prevention." Detection of what? Prevention of what? As I kept walking, I noticed more little signs along the way showing footprints and arrows. And then I saw them – a group of women wearing pink shirts. And it finally hit me. *Of course! It's the March for Breast Cancer Awareness – and the guy is filming it – and he's wearing a pink tutu in solidarity. It makes perfect sense!*

That "aha moment" allowed my brain to relax, for I was suddenly in a state of "coherence." Now that my brain could understand what my eyes were seeing, I could create a mental construct, an explanatory story that made sense because until the pieces of the picture fell into place, my brain - that little meaning-making, story-telling machine - was out of sorts.

Finding Meaning in the Chaos

In this particular instance, my confusion was very short-lived. More often, however, there are times in our lives, periods that can last for years or a lifetime, in which we lack that coherence, where life events seem tragically painful or incomprehensibly sad. At those times, when we are left holding pieces of a puzzle that don't seem to fit, we are most challenged to trust that such a coherent picture actually does exist.

Perhaps we are simply not seeing the missing pieces, and we need to look harder or search with a new set of eyes. Failing that, we can choose to view life as chaotic and meaningless, or we can come to believe that the seemingly disconnected fragments of our life nevertheless make up a unified whole, and that like the proverbial back of a tapestry, one day its beauty will reveal itself to us. You could say it's the long view of life – the very long view.

In *Vayeishev*, we read the familiar story of Joseph, who goes from enjoying the prestige of being Jacob's favorite son (good) to being thrown into a pit by his brothers and ultimately sold as a slave to Potiphar (bad). Joseph, however, quickly rose to become Potiphar's #2 (good), but when Potiphar's wife falsely accused Joseph of attempted rape, he was back in the pit of prison again (bad). Ultimately Joseph becomes Pharaoh's #2 (good) and saves and reunites his family (very good).

Taken separately, each aspect of the Joseph story is extreme, either painfully heartrending or appearing to defy reason, unfolding in a cosmic "aha" that has reverberated for millennia. As Viktor E. Frankl explains:

> Consider a movie: it consists of thousands upon thousands of individual pictures, and each of them makes sense and carries a meaning, yet the meaning of the whole film cannot be seen before its last sequence is shown. However, we cannot understand the whole film without having first understood each of its components, each of the individual pictures. Isn't it the same with life? Doesn't the final meaning of life, too, reveal itself, if at all, only at its end, on the verge of death?[18]

Attaining a state of coherence gives us more than a happy brain. It is fundamental to our very well-being and ability to cope with the stressors and challenges of life. In between those moments of revelation when suddenly everything makes sense, is the challenge to cling to the belief that sense is there to be made, revealed in the next moment, the next year, at the end of life or even over the course of the lifetimes. Continues Frankl, "This is the core of the human spirit.... If we can find something to live for - if we can find some meaning to put at the center of our lives - even the worst kind of suffering becomes bearable."

1. Write about a challenging and difficult time in your life that ultimately led to positive healing, growth or change. What emotions did you experience when it was happening? At the time, could you see any good coming from it? Then write what happened that ultimately stemmed from that seemingly negative experience. What emotions do you now feel when you look back at both experiences as part of a package deal?

    _____

    _____

    _____

2. Based on the situation above, what aspects of yourself and strengths have emerged from this process? How are you a different person because of what happened than you were before you had to face this challenge?

   _____

   _____

   _____

3. Think now about something you are struggling with. What are your fears? What emotions are evoked when dealing with this? Now write about this situation from the future. In 5, 10 or 15 years, looking back, will this still be an issue? Will this even have an impact on your future and if so, in what ways?

   _____

   _____

   _____

OH, THE LIES WE TELL

(*Mikeitz*/Genesis 41:1 – 44:17)

"Reality blithely ignores the lies we tell ourselves about it."

- Chris Cogan

The most touching moment in stories where loved ones are reunited is that instant flash of recognition they have for each other, despite the years or even decades that may have intervened. So, I always wondered how it was possible when Joseph's brothers went down to Egypt and saw Joseph, and even approached him up close, that they did not know who it was – after all, it had only been 13 years the brothers had seen him last.

In describing that encounter, the text recounts: "Joseph recognized his brothers, but they did not recognize him."[19] True, Joseph was now the Viceroy of Egypt – an unlikely context for the young brother they had sold into slavery - but still, not even a glimmer of uncertainty, or questioning an uncanny physical resemblance?

Why We Forget the Wrongdoings of Our Past – Unethical Amnesia

In a psychological phenomenon known as "Unethical Amnesia," people have a tendency to forget the details of their transgressions. Says Francesco Gino, of Harvard Business School, "We are social beings, and our basic need for self-worth is affected by moral self-views. Unethical behavior creates psychological distress and discomfort, and unethical amnesia lowers it."[20] While unethical amnesia would explain a hazy recollection of the details and motives surrounding the incident, it wouldn't obliterate their memory of Joseph entirely.

To be fair, by what stretch of the imagination could anyone imagine that the brother that was sold to a passing caravan of Ishmaelites could wind up as Pharaoh's Second in Command? On the other hand, maybe the thought never occurred to the brothers because such a thought could lead to something dangerous – like an "Inconvenient Truth."

Because if the impossible were to become possible and even true, then what would that say about the brothers' underlying assumptions and motives to get rid of Joseph in the first place? After all, when it bumps up against the constructs we create and the stories we make up, truth can be quite inconvenient. As Kierkegaard said, "We fool ourselves into believing lies and we refuse to believe things that are true." Joseph's brothers were unable to see the truth staring them in the face. How often do we make the same mistake?

Eight Common Lies[21]

1. We lie about the seemingly inconsequential things – "I'll just call in sick at work."
2. And we lie about significant things – like ourselves, who we really are at the core. That makes us play small and avoid risks. "I could never...."
3. We lie when we blame others and defend ourselves. "I wouldn't have to yell at you if you just listened to me!"
4. And we lie when we project by taking the undesirable and conflicted aspects of ourselves and put them on someone else. "I'm not like that – you're like that!"
5. We lie when we think in extremes. "I can't ever eat cookies because if I eat even just one single cookie, I will wind up eating the whole box of cookies. Oh darn, I just ate a cookie...."
6. We lie when we minimize the good things about our loved ones, and the positivity in our lives and the world as a whole.

7. And we lie when we hyper focus on and maximize the bad. These, in particular, are the lies that suck the joy out of life and rob relationships of their potential.

8. We have the lie of our feelings. We think if we feel something, if we have a particular emotion, then by golly, it must be true. I "feel" hurt - so you must have done something wrong to me. I "feel" stupid - so I must be.

What is the cost of all this self-deception? When we don't recognize the truth, or take full responsibility for who we are, we don't just hurt ourselves – we hurt everyone around us. It's toxic. And it spreads. So how can we clean up our act?

Seeing Truth Is a Choice

When we become more internally aware and critically evaluate our thoughts, we can begin to recognize truth and drop the stories that sap us of our vitality and the ability to connect. We become more honest about our thoughts, and thereby, become more responsible for our choices. We also understand better the arena of choice, in that the only thing we can truly control is our reaction to that which is completely out of our control.

Recognizing truth is a life-long process. Lift one illusory veil, and there is sure to be another right behind it – but it won't be the same veil. And that's the point, for as Rilke said, "The purpose of life is to be defeated by greater and greater things." And so, the pursuit of truth is an unending discovery of deeper and deeper realities.

Joseph's brothers could not recognize Joseph because, at this point, they were still too attached to the lies they told themselves to rationalize their behavior. They were still standing by the story they created to give themselves permission to do what they did, and they couldn't admit a reality that would obliterate their whole construct. And so, they were blind to the truth standing before them. Seeing the truth is a choice. "It is also," says American author Marty Rubin, "an act of courage." Admitting the truth of what we see, furthermore, is an act of strength.

Internalize & Actualize:

1. What are the lies you have told yourself because it was easier to believe an untruth, than to deal with the truth? Write down three situations where you continue to do this:

    Three lies you tell yourself:

    _____

    _____

    _____

2. What is the cost of believing these false stories? What are you trying to avoid by sticking to these lies rather than admit what you know to be true?

    Cost /What you are avoiding?

    _____

    _____

    _____

3. Write down some practical ways you can start to undo the lies by facing the truth directly. This can be your thought, speech or action (the "garments of your soul" as previously discussed). Then, begin to implement your insights and write down how you feel as you engage these things you have avoided. Make sure to date your entries so you can watch your progress unfold.

    Practical ways to face the truth:

    _____

    _____

    _____

THE POWER OF STORY IN OUR LIVES

(*Vayigash*/Genesis 44:18 – 47:27)

*"You don't just have a story - you're a story in the making
and you never know what the next chapter's going to be.
That's what makes it exciting."*

- Dan Millman

It's said that human beings can live a few weeks without food, a few days without water, but only about 30 seconds without finding meaning in something. Creating stories is what we naturally do. Stories are not the problem. After all, we are hard-wired for story; it's how we make sense of everyone and everything.

But we live in the stories we create. And so, the challenge, therefore, is to create stories that work for us instead of against us, and to write the stories of our lives in ways that are empowering, strengths-based and growth-oriented, instead of victim-based, disempowering and fueled by shame.

Coming into a State of Coherence

The first stories we tell about ourselves form what is referred to as "the narrative arc of our lives." Aaron Antonovsky, one of the pioneers of medical sociology, was able to correlate the connection between having a strong sense of narrative coherence and greater happiness, health, resilience and motivation to take positive action. Thus, coherence is not just a "nicety;" in fact, our very well-being depends on it. Says Antonovsky, three elements contribute to a strong sense of coherence:[22]

1. **Comprehensibility**. I understand what has happened (or is going on in my life). My important life stories make sense to me.

2. **Manageability**. I can cope with what has happened (or is happening) in my life. It's not easy, but I can summon the internal and external resources I need to manage my life.

3. **Meaningfulness**. I have grown or learned (or have the potential to) as a result of my experiences. The challenges I face are worth addressing.

"*Vayigash*" is a perfect example of what is possible when one is in a state of "coherence." The story of Joseph and his brothers reaches its climax with one of the most dramatic moments in Biblical narrative. In reaction to Joseph's feigned refusal to release Benjamin, Yehuda begged Joseph to take him in Benjamin's stead, pleading that the loss of another son – *this son* - would kill his father, Jacob.

Unable to restrain himself any longer, Joseph burst out revealing his true identity, stating, "*Ani Yosef*," "I am Joseph!" The brothers were in shock and terrified. Before them stood the complete refutation of their actions, against which they were utterly defenseless. As the Viceroy of Egypt, Joseph could have them imprisoned or worse, but miraculously, he bore the brothers no ill will. Not only was Joseph *not* punitive, but he even comforted his brothers; a gesture that was both compassionate and empowering, whereby Joseph stripped the brothers of the notion that they had ever had any actual control over his fate.

The Bigger Picture

For underneath the surface drama of the story, and the intentions and motives of the brothers, is an omniscient, omnipresent and omnipotent God, who was orchestrating events to fulfill a Divine plan. This belief in the bigger picture and deeper meaning of otherwise meaningless and tragic events gave Joseph a sense of purpose, helping him to manage and cope with his ordeals and remain spiritually, emotionally and mentally intact. How else could he emerge from twelve years in an Egyptian prison with all of his wits about him, so as to be promoted to Viceroy of Egypt on the spot!

Whether it was at that very moment, or later, when he finally saw his brothers, his story "made sense," became "comprehensible" and Joseph was able to narrate it in a way that was empowering. Rather than be a victim, consumed with hatred and bitterness, Joseph was filled with strength and grace.

Telling a New Story

In her book, *Wired for Story*,[23] Lisa Cron explains how a plot is what *happens*, whereas the real story is how the protagonist *changes* in reaction to the plot. Understandably, the plot hooks us, but the purpose of the story is much deeper than the mere telling of events. Looking below the storyline of "what happened" to get at "what the story was about," affords us a new perspective. When we look at the painful stories of our past and see how we nevertheless coped and managed, and how we were able to transmute suffering into growth, then the stories of our lives can take on new meanings, meanings that can even make some overall sense. This awareness of coherence then gives us the strength and resilience to deal with the struggles and challenges of our present.

And that fills us with well-being, optimism, and possibility. Our challenge is to stop telling the stories that keep us stuck in blame. Like Joseph, we can compose the narratives of our past in ways that are empowering, and in so doing, we can use our past to inspire our present and to inform a better future.[24] When we can look back at the events of our past and embrace them as being the perfect training ground for who we are today, then we can begin to be the authors of our own lives.

Internalize & Actualize:

1. We all have stories that we create and which we think of as objective truth. Think of a time when someone wronged you, and you felt betrayed. Now, retell that story to yourself but exonerate that person. Say or write it in a way where the person was not trying to hurt you and/or was unaware that he/she was doing so. Make this person innocent in your new version. Then, respond to the following: how does this new story make you feel? How do you now feel about this person?

   Retelling of story
   How do you feel? How do you feel towards that person?

   _____
   _____
   _____

2. Write down three situations where you feel you successfully overcame a difficulty. What qualities came out of you in those situations that helped you to be successful (i.e. patience, empathy, self-awareness, etc.)?

   Three successful situations:
   List your qualities in those situations:

   _____
   _____
   _____

3. Write down a challenge you are facing right now. Think about the qualities you just listed which you know you are capable of tapping into. Which of these will help you through your current challenge? How can you implement it/them to work through a challenge?

   Current challenge/quality from above that can help you and how:

   _____
   _____
   _____

HOW TO SEE THE GOOD
ALL AROUND YOU

(*Vayechi*/Genesis 47:28 – 50:26)

"Everything changes when you see challenges as blessings."

- Anonymous

In Hebrew, every letter has a numerical equivalent. So, each word has a number associated with it, derived by adding up the value of the letters of that word. For example, the first letter in the Hebrew alphabet has the numerical equivalent of "1," and the second letter equals "2," and so on. This process, known as *"gematria,"* reveals incredible insights, wherein words and phrases that don't otherwise seem related, nevertheless are, because of their numerical equivalents.

When the Torah introduces us to Joseph,[25] the first thing we learn about him is that he was 17 years old at the time he was sold into slavery. Note the occurrences of the number "17." The name of the Torah portion, *"Vayechi,"* means *"and he lived,"* and this refers to the period comprised of the last 17 years of Jacob's life, in which he spent living in Egypt, where he was reunited with his beloved son, Joseph. Thus, like bookends, Jacob lived with Joseph for two exact time periods: the first 17 years of his son's life, and then again for the last 17 years of Jacob's life.

The numerical equivalent of the Hebrew word, "*Vayechi,*" is "34," which is 17 x 2. Furthermore, the Hebrew word for "good" is "*tov,*" and that word also has the numerical equivalent of "17." Even if you are not a math geek, don't switch off your brain – stay with me here.

From this, we can infer that these two specific 17-year periods of Jacob's life, the ones in which he lived with Joseph were considered "good," and were, in fact, the "years of his life," meaning, the years when he felt most joyful and alive. Jacob died at age 147, however, and so what was the quality of the rest of his life in between these years? Life is not always lived in the peak moments; we have to navigate the numerous valleys as well.

Complaining is a Killer

While Jacob had a lot of challenges, he certainly didn't corner the market on suffering. However, upon being introduced to the Pharaoh, Pharaoh asked Jacob why he looked so "old," and Jacob complained about his life. *Each* word of complaint (thirty-three in all) supposedly shortened his lifespan by a year, meaning that Jacob lost 37 years off of his supposed lifespan.

Perhaps Jacob was being punished for expressing "lack" instead of "abundance" in the face of being reunited with the son he long thought was dead. After all, when someone knocks you to the ground - but you unexpectedly find a huge diamond in the dirt - do you still complain about the shove? How could there have been for room for any complaints at that moment?

In contrast, when Joseph had ultimately revealed himself to his brothers, they were, understandably, terrified to be in his presence. Nevertheless, Joseph comforted them by saying that whatever their intentions were, it was God's plan that the events unfolded exactly as they did – for this purpose, for this reason, for this moment.[26] Therefore Joseph harbored no ill will; after all, when you don't see yourself as a victim, it's impossible to hold a grudge. While he certainly would have had every reason and right to do so, Joseph uttered not one word of complaint.

Seeing the Good

Viktor Frankl observed that a sense of meaning ameliorates suffering. While Jacob "came back to life," when he was reunited with Joseph, there is no sense that Jacob experienced that "aha" moment, that sense of coherence obtained in the moment of meaning that transforms suffering, and so, Jacob's anguish all those prior years remained the same – meaningless suffering.

So how can we emulate and tap into being like Joseph? How can we open our eyes and see more "*tov,*" more "*good*" in our own lives, regardless of our challenges and the minor and major shoves in our lives? How can we shift the meaningless to the meaningful?

When you experience a state of coherence, that is, when the stories of your life make sense, it creates "aha moments" over the events of your past. Whereas, before, you had mere stories of plot, that such and such happened; suddenly, you begin to see connections within the stories and in between the stories. You start to see narratives in a new light, and therefore, the old stories become new stories.

You even wonder - how had I missed such meaning? How had I failed to connect the dots? How had I not seen the evolution, the blessings, the transformations – that could *only* have happened the way that they did, each thread weaving inexorably into the next? "Failure is only failure if it happens in the last chapter – otherwise, it's a plot twist."[27]

Like those fun picture books we had as children, where we traced outlines following the numbers and were delighted when a picture suddenly revealed itself; coherence is becoming aware how the dots connect to reveal an image we finally can understand. When that happens, a new sense of Divine benevolence and providence surfaces; whereas, before there had only been story – "victim story," "problem story," "trauma story," etc.

Eventually, we can learn to be the authors of our own life. Coherence is a choice. Since we always see what we are looking for, the more "*tov*" we look for, the more "good" we will see. As Tal Ben-Shahar, "the Happiness Professor from Harvard," likes to quip: "Appreciate the good – and the good appreciates." May we see all of the numerous "17's" around us – in whatever guise they may appear - and like the righteous Joseph, no matter what our challenges and hardships, may we nevertheless see the whole of our lives as "*tov*/good."

Internalize & Actualize:

1. Think about three things that have happened in your life that you would define as negative or bad. Write them down and alongside them write down what feelings you associate with them (pain, hurt, anger, fear, etc.).

    Three negative things / feelings associated:

    _____

    _____

    _____

2. Now, for each of these three things, write down at least three positive lessons or outcomes that resulted from the negative situation. They can be things that only happened well after the fact (e.g., I was devastated when I was fired, but two years later I landed my dream job and would not have been available had I still been working with my old company, etc.).

    Three positive outcomes:

    _____

    _____

    _____

3. This week experiment how being in a positive frame of mind will influence your day and those around you. Implement the following throughout your week and then write down how others reacted and how it made you feel. Smile at people you pass on the street and see how many smile back. Compliment a few strangers on something small - "I love your scarf," or "That is a really nice tie." Make an effort to "see" the positive things happening around you. Write down a few things each day that you noticed because

you paid attention (a stranger held the door open for you, a new line opened when the cashier saw you waiting, you watched a teenager help an old lady cross the street, etc.).

Reactions to Smile / Compliment / See the good:

_____

_____

_____

-SHEMOT-
EXODUS

THE *WHO* OF WHO YOU ARE

(*Shemot*/Exodus 1:1 – 6:1)

"The privilege of a lifetime is to become who you truly are."

- C.G. Jung

Like most children, I was taught that lying is bad. When I got older, however, I realized that some people, especially those who like to pat themselves on the back for their "honesty," can be quite cruel; hence the term – "the brutal truth." In such cases, "honesty" can be a tad overrated. On the other hand, when we lie, the disconnect and lack of any congruence we create stands in the way of the potential of relationships, and the fulfillment of our destiny.

The Search for Authenticity

These days, many of us search for honesty in the form of "authenticity." We want to be true to ourselves, while also letting people into our private world, and allow them to see us for who we are. However, for those of us who have worn our personae well, perhaps for decades, the thought of dropping the mask and authentically connecting with others can be scary. Embracing the vulnerability of connection can be treading new water for many; yet, it can also be exhilarating with the promise of a new paradigm.

But really, who are we anyway? Deep down, who is the *who* of who we are? And let's face it; is honesty or authenticity always the best policy? Speaking personally, some aspects of my character are far from polished and are in fact, not so nice. Whether it's my sarcastic, judgmental, or impatient self, I am pretty good sometimes, at being a little awful. For better or worse, these qualities nevertheless show up as part of my "authentic self." So, do I lift the curtain to reveal the "whole enchilada" me? And if so, is authenticity nothing more than a challenge to "take me as I am?"

The Three Prongs of Authenticity

No. Authenticity is not a be-all and end-all concept; rather it is a three-pronged construct of authenticity, integrity, and servant/leadership that comprises a state of "wholeness." By definition, "wholeness" cannot be a disconnected and self-centered state of being; "wholeness" is a unifying force based on connection and interconnection. So, while we can manifest and lead from any aspect of ourselves, even the negative ones, and still be within the parameters of "authenticity," "wholeness" asks us not to do that. Authenticity tells us to look within. Authenticity acknowledges multiple authentic and sometimes incompatible realities. Wholeness, on the other hand, asks us to consider the bigger picture and the external impact we are choosing to make. And wholeness asks us to choose which of those realities we want to make operational in any given moment. In this week's Torah portion, "*Shemot,*" Moses famously encounters the "Burning Bush:"

> The angel of the Lord appeared to him in a blazing fire from the midst of a bush; and he looked, and behold, the bush was burning with fire, yet the bush was not consumed. So Moses said, "I must turn aside now and see this marvelous sight, why the bush is not burned up." When the Lord saw that he turned aside to look, God called to him from the midst of the bush and said, "Moses, Moses!" And he said, "Here I am."[28]

Some commentators focus on the fact that it was a lowly thorn bush, thus emphasizing the attribute of "humility," marveling that God would appear in something so inconsequential. Others interpret the "blazing fire that does not consume" to mean that even when our enemies try to destroy, obliterate and burn us, the Jewish people will never be totally consumed by the fire of hatred.

Incompatible Realities

These views focus on one aspect or the other of the Burning Bush. What I find most fascinating, however, is the paradox of it, the exquisite harmony of totally incompatible realities – a burning bush - that is not being consumed. Walt Whitman famously wrote, "I contain multitudes." And thus, we are all "Burning Bushes" in that we all contain within us the paradox of multiple and incompatible realities that form one holistic whole.

Parker Palmer, an educator, author and activist, explains it thus: "In certain circumstances, truth is not found by splitting the world into either-or but by embracing it as both–and."[29] And so, if you are *only* a bush or *only* fire, then you are acting from only one perspective, and you are missing the wholeness, the totality of being a "burning bush." While some situations call for quiet humility and others for blazing fire, it is all one authentic you. The point is to know when to be what, and how you can act from your highest self. That would be the prong of integrity.

The Power of Servant/Leadership

Moses wanted to serve God and, at the same time, he was also terrified that he was not up to the task. He had two mindsets going on, but one choice to make. Moses embraced his fear, acknowledged that truth (the prong of authenticity), but then acted from the self that wanted to serve God. That is the moment when he stepped into the prong of servant/leader.

And so, authenticity is not about being an indiscriminate open book without orders or boundaries. Nor is it an excuse for causing pain and suffering to others. "Authenticity," says Scott Edmund Miller, "is the act of openly and courageously seeing what needs to be seen, saying what needs to be said, doing what needs to be done, and becoming that which you are intent on being."

So be authentic. By all means, be who you are in your full paradoxical and multitudinous self. But remember, that in the *who* of who you are, there is *always* a choice. In your quest for authenticity be guided by integrity and be inspired by servant/leadership. Be mindful. Be kind. And be whole.

Internalize and Actualize:

1. Write down five descriptions of yourself that you know to be authentically true. Do you think these descriptions are positive or negative? Underneath that list write down five descriptions that others have of you. Which of these do you believe to be true?

    five authentically true descriptions (positive or negative):
    five descriptions others have of you:

    _____

    _____

    _____

2. List the people with whom you can be completely yourself. Would they agree that the qualities that you think are negative are true or negative? If not, how do they see that quality? Do they see it as positive or with positive potential?

    People with whom you are authentic:
    How they see your "negative" and authentic qualities:

    _____

    _____

    _____

3. Ideally, you can reach a point where you do not hide your authentic qualities and the ways that others see you will also be in alignment with who you are. How can you begin to integrate the two? For example, if others see you as strong and powerful, but you see yourself as insecure and sensitive, how can the two work together to benefit you? Are there times where showing your vulnerability would help others see that you are not perfect and respect your strength even more? Write down how you think it would make you feel to be more honest and authentic with others and not put up a front.

    Ways to integrate what you know and what others think:
    How will this make you feel (and after you have tried, how does this make you feel?)

WHY MAKING REDEMPTION A DAILY HABIT IS GOOD FOR YOU AND YOUR RELATIONSHIPS

(Va'eira/Exodus 6:2 – 9:35)

"The way you remember the past depends upon your hope for the future."

– Story Musgrave

One sure way to make people avoid you is if you continue to live in the past and refuse to move on from a painful experience. Catching a cheating spouse will certainly garner sympathy, but if it's been years and the infidelity is still an on-going complaint, your circle of friends may whittle down to like-minded whiners. Even the Book of Ecclesiastes urges us to move on. "To everything there is a season"[30] can be seen as a Biblical exhortation to "go with the flow" or "get over it!"

Many Jews, however, recite daily the "Six Remembrances,"[31] one of which is to "remember the day when you went out of the land of Egypt all the days of your life."[32] For starters, I already have enough on my plate in the morning. Besides, we do this anyway at great length during the Passover Seder – so why ruminate about it daily? Taking a page from the process known as "Appreciative Inquiry,"[33] when we draw strength from the past, we can inform a present reality that will inspire a better future.

In *Va'eira*, God tells Moses the *four* ways that He will redeem the

Jewish people. First, redemption is not a one-step and one-direction process. Exiting the narrow spiritual confines of Egypt allowed us to go towards the expansiveness of connection and service to God. Leaving negativity is not an end unto itself but a precursor to embracing positivity. And that's not a once and done event but rather an inquiry and reflection into the false mental constructs that enslave us for our entire lives. If you are having trouble making the positive changes you want for yourself and your relationships, it may pay to look at each component of the 4-step redemptive process:

1. **"I shall take you out from under the burdens."**
   Commit to Stopping.

This step refers to God stopping the hard labor. While the Ten Plagues occurred over a period of time, the physical burden of slavery came to an end well before the Jews left Egypt. Therefore, when you want to shift a pattern of negative behavior, you have to genuinely full-out commit to stopping it and not repeating it. I cannot stress enough that if you find yourself unable to refrain from repeating old patterns, honestly check whether you have placed a high enough value on the change you want to see.

2. **"I shall rescue you."**
   Avoid temptation and have a strategy.

This step refers to God taking us out of the very land of Egypt. So, if you can circumvent the situations that tempt you, you should. Weight Watchers has a great saying to help people avoid buying groceries that contain forbidden food items – "Don't bring your enemies home with you." But seriously, the key to the adopting of any new behavior is having a strategy for dealing with that which *inevitably* gets in the way.

3. **"I shall redeem you."**
   Look under the hood.

This refers to the deeper levels of our mental schema. It's one thing to take a Jew out of Egypt but quite another to take Egypt out of the Jew.

The Jewish people had to be rebuilt from the ground up, to unlearn the internal constructs of slavery, to "upgrade their operating system" and to understand what it means to be truly holy.

"Fake it till you make it" is a methodology whereby if you keep doing something externally, eventually it will become an internal reality. Truthfully, I've never had much luck with that. And if you are having real difficulty in realizing your goals, you may need to get to the root of the hidden beliefs and the fears that are blocking you. Unless you tune into the whispers of your inner voices, you can get very frustrated and not even know why. Having trouble with making a positive change doesn't mean you are a loser or incapable of change. It does suggest, however, that you need to figure it out, and I stand for the proposition that it's all *figureoutable*.

4.   **"I shall take you to Me for a people."**
     Step into your higher purpose.

If you saw the movie *The Matrix*, when the humans finally won the war against the machines, they all broke out into a frenzied delirium of physical gratification. And *then* what was supposed to happen? Freedom is not the same as a free-for-all. In taking us out of Egypt, the real challenge was to create a new relationship between man and God.

On my desk sits a framed quote by Thoreau: "Be not simply good; be good for something." As you begin to incorporate a new positive change in your life, it's not a stand-alone idea. If your goal is to be more loving in a relationship, then see how many different ways you can make a person feel cherished by you. Look for the means to broaden and share your process and purpose. Allow it to evolve into higher and higher goals. Create a vision. Live with purpose. Make a difference.

Internalize & Actualize:

1.   Think about a bad habit you have that you want to stop. Then write down the circumstances that tend to occur when you are most likely to do this bad habit. You will find that at least some of these circumstances are avoidable. Write down practical steps

you can take to avoid the situations that tempt you to do this bad habit. Over the next few weeks, pay attention if you are less likely to do it when you are no longer in the situations that support it.

_____

_____

_____

2. Now that you are more aware of the situations you want to avoid where you are likely to do this bad habit, let's deal with the bad habit directly. Has this habit had an adverse impact on anyone else around you? If so, can you apologize to that person and let them know you are working on this? How else has this habit had a negative impact on your life? Write down a few steps you can take to help rectify any damage it may have already done.

_____

_____

_____

3. Whatever your negative habit, you can offset it with a counter positive activity. It is not enough to just stop something undesirable; ideally, you want to replace the bad habit with a good one. Think about what you can do that would directly relate to the activity or behavior that you want to avoid, that could then be done to counter or even transform the negative.

_____

_____

_____

15

THE BALANCING ACT OF FREEDOM – KNOWING WHEN TO BE WHAT

(*Bo*/Exodus 10:1 – 13:16)

"I believe now that our fractured society is longing for a world in which the unity of humanity and the cosmos, the wholeness of body, soul and spirit and the unity of the masculine and feminine principles is valued, in which meaning is restored."

- Chris Clark

In all honesty, who among you doesn't over pack? Or have a hard time getting out of the house? Even though my husband and I were going on a mere 3-day excursion to New York, which is seriously the land of everything 24/7, you would think by the amount of luggage we had that we were going on a Sherpa-assisted expedition to the Himalayas. We left home an hour and a half past our estimated departure time (don't ask). Ten minutes into the trip we had to turn around and come back home to get a forgotten item (really, don't ask). And I couldn't help but wonder how Moses managed to get a few million Jews and all of their possessions, out of Egypt in one fell swoop.

In the Torah portion, "*Bo,*" we see the unfolding of the last three plagues, the laws of Passover and the leaving of Egypt. That's a lot of stuff for Moses to be dealing with, and so I was curious about the insertion of two lines that seemed really incongruous. God said to Moses and Aaron:

"This month shall be for you the beginning of the months. It shall be for you the first of the months of the year."[34] Embedded in these two cryptic lines is the command to sanctify the new moon (*Rosh Chodesh*) and also to ensure that Passover always occurs in the spring season.

Controlling Time

In essence, in the middle of one of the biggest and craziest events in history, God commanded Moses to create a "calendar" – and not just any calendar – but a strange and unique calendar that is based on both the lunar months and the solar year. These two systems (lunar and solar) are not in sync, however, and thus an extra month is added to certain years, and other adjustments are made to reconcile the two over a perpetual 19-year cycle. What was so important about this that it had to be commanded on the eve of leaving Egypt - and why make it so complicated?

The Hebrew word for Egypt is *"Mitzrayim,"* from the word *"meitzar"* – which means "narrow" and "constricted." In leaving Egypt, the Jewish people were going from narrowness to expansion, from a bounded country to a limitless open desert, and from slavery to freedom.

One of the hallmarks of being a slave is the inability to control anything, specifically time. When God commanded us to be in charge of publicly announcing the new moon (*Rosh Chodesh*/the new month), we were given the gift of being able to declare and sanctify time itself. And as the Jewish people were coming into their newly liberated status, it was important that they understood that freedom is not the same as a "free-for-all" and that expansion and freedom requires a balanced approach.

Masculine and Feminine Energy

Jewish mysticism teaches us that the differences between the sun and the moon are not just physical, but spiritual and that the masculine spiritual energy of giving (the sun) and the feminine spiritual energy of receiving (the moon) are two cosmic forces that need to be brought into balance and harmony.

Typically, masculine energy emits its energy in a "top-down" and proactive way. When masculine power interacts with the world, the predominant energy is the execution of will upon something or someone. The characteristics of feminine energy, on the other hand, are "bottom-up" and receptive. When feminine energy interacts with the world, the emphasis is on revealing potential, cultivating and transforming.

This is *not* about being a man or a woman. Rather, these are energies and qualities that we all have, and it goes back to the beginning, with the creation of Adam, that occurred in two parts. First, as a being created in the image of God, Adam was given dominion over everything. If it crawled, walked, swam or flew, Adam was in charge. This was proactive masculine energy. Second, when God blew His breath into Adam's nostrils, placed him in the Garden of Eden and told him to "tend it," Adam was tasked with being a caretaker, cultivating and nurturing. This was feminine energy. We need both energies, both ways of being – but to be a free and fully functioning person, we need to know "when to be what."

The Right Time for Everything

There are times when we need an immediate solution to something, where there is a crisis, calling for a fast and effective leadership. And there are times when leadership serves by building consensus, collaborative brainstorming, building relationships and cultivating talent. There are times when we need to impart concepts and information, and times when we want to foster the process of learning. There is a time to be active and a time to be passive. There is a time to be the conqueror and a time to be the cultivator. There is a time to be Adam #1 and Adam #2.[35]

In the book, *Built to Last*,[36] authors Collins and Porras conducted a six-year study at the Stanford University Graduate School of Business, studying eighteen truly exceptional and long-lasting companies as well as their direct competitors. They were looking for an answer to the question: "What makes the truly exceptional companies different from the comparison companies and what were the common practices these enduringly great companies followed throughout their history?" In other words, was there a secret to their success?

And what they found was that exceptional companies all shared this trait in common – they knew "when to be what." They knew when to be hierarchical and when to be flat, when to micro-manage and when to full-out delegate. They had a fixed core of values as well as the flexibility to change on a dime. By being able to embrace both sides of the coin, they knew "what to do when" and "when to be what." Jewish mysticism teaches that the era of redemption will see the return of feminine energy. Masculine energy can win a war and in an external and top-down manner, impose a cease-fire. True peace, however, "shalom," "wholeness," is an organic, bottom-up and internal process. In the times of the Messiah, said the prophet Isaiah, "the light of the moon shall be like the light of the sun."[37] Thus, these cosmic forces and energies will be in balance and harmony.

When we left Egypt, we received the Torah and we were tasked with being the light unto nations. We have to be conscious of our ability to receive and our strength to give. We must be conscious of our collective soul as well as our individual missions, and to bring our families, our communities, the world and ultimately ourselves into a state of balance. When the whole world knows "when to be what," the sun and moon will be equal. Says Rabbi David Aaron, "To each and every one of us there are two faces to our inner selves, but they are really two halves of one coin. If we understand and appreciate this fact, then those two sides which seem to be in conflict can instead become a source of tremendous life force."[38]

Internalize & Actualize:

1. Has there been a situation, which you met with a forceful and decisive energy, which could have been better served if you had met it with a nurturing and receptive energy? How about the reverse? List at least one situation from each.

   _____

   _____

   _____

2. Is there a situation right now, which would benefit from your immediate attention and action? What do you need to be doing

right now that you are avoiding taking on? Which approach do you want to take and does that differ from which approach you *should* take?

_____

_____

_____

3. Think about your hesitation to either tap into the more active, top-down approach or the more passive, bottom-up approach. Where do you think that hesitation comes from? Do you assign the roles to gender (e.g. you feel you are being too manly if you do things a certain way, etc.)? Write down five ways you could incorporate the less natural approach to you that you feel would improve and benefit these areas in your life (e.g. being more assertive when speaking to co-workers, not criticizing as much when children/ spouse are admitting a mistake, etc.)

_____

_____

_____

16

IS YOUR OPTIMISM GROUNDED IN REALITY?

*(Beshalach/*Exodus 13:17 – 17:16)

"The pessimist sees the difficulty in every opportunity; the optimist sees the opportunity in every difficulty."

- Winston Churchill

A man gets into his car and decides – in the name of "optimism" – that he won't buckle up. Is he an optimist or is he foolish? After delivering a lecture on optimism to a large tech company, Shawn Achor, an international speaker on Positive Psychology, was being driven to the airport by the CEO. Ignoring the persistent and annoying dinging of the alarm for not using his seat belt, the CEO smiled at Shawn and explained that he was just being "optimistic." "Optimism is good for a lot of things," thought Shawn, "but it will not prevent this CEO from getting into a car accident, nor will it prevent him flying through the windshield."[39] This is not optimism; rather, it's a form of insanity, otherwise known as "irrational optimism."

In the Torah portion, *"Beshalach,"* after the Jewish people left Egypt, Pharaoh set loose his army of charioteers after them, and the Jewish people were cornered with Egypt at their back, the vast desert on both sides and the sea in front of them. Short of a new miracle, the Jewish people were facing imminent slaughter.

The Splitting of the Sea

According to rabbinic commentary, some people wanted to surrender and go back to Egypt. Some were ready to commit suicide. Some were willing to fight the Egyptians. And another group started to pray. Moses cried out to God and God replied (in essence) – "Stop praying and journey forth – *do something!*" It was at that point that the famous Nachshon ben Aminadav jumped into the sea, and when the water reached his nostrils, the sea began to part. Was he an optimist or insane? Irrational or grounded?

In his book, "Learned Optimism,"[40] Martin Seligman, known as the father of Positive Psychology, explains that there are two ways of looking at life - as an optimist and as a pessimist - and he gives an example. A young couple has their first baby. The father looks at her in her crib and he calls out her name. Although the baby is awake, she doesn't respond. Dad picks up a toy with a bell and shakes it. No response. Dad's heart starts to beat rapidly, and he summons his wife. The mother was also unable to get the baby's attention with loud sounds. "My God, she's deaf," concludes the father.

Mom consults a baby book for advice, reading how there is no reason for alarm since it takes time for the startle and sound reflex to kick in. Mom is reassured. Nevertheless, she leaves a voice message with the pediatrician's office to schedule an appointment, and she goes about her weekend as usual. Dad, on the other hand, remains a worried mess, ruminating that he has a "bad feeling about this."

On Monday, the pediatrician administers a neurological exam and finds the baby perfectly healthy. Father does not believe the test results and still remains depressed and worried. A week later, when the baby startled at the noise of a backfiring car, the father began to recover his spirits and was able to enjoy his baby once again.

Says Seligman, the pessimist "awfulizes" events, views harmful situations as long-lasting, if not permanent, allows the upset to permeate all areas of life and takes it personally. The optimist, on the other hand, doesn't anticipate defeat, but when it happens, sees defeat as a challenge to be surmounted, limits it to this pertinent situation, and sees the cause as something external.

Okay, now it's a little chutzpadich, but I think there is another explanatory style, which I am calling "Jewish Optimism," and since I'm coining the phrase, I get to define it. "Jewish Optimism" takes the best aspects of optimism, such as looking at events in their most favorable light and rising to the challenge with an "I-can" or an "it-can-be-done" attitude.

But when it comes to causality, "Jewish Optimism" would not regard events as external and impersonal. Just the opposite. In "Jewish Optimism," everything is "about me" – for my spiritual growth, that is. And this brings in the quality of faith - faith that the universe is not out to "get me," but to "teach me."

Getting back to the scene at the banks of the Sea of Reeds, in facing Pharaoh's army, the same God that liberated the Jewish people through His open and Divine intervention was now telling them to go, to "*do something*." Nachshon, the Jewish optimist, walked calmly into the sea, and in so doing, he also paved the way for the Jewish expression of faith.

This sets Judaism apart from any religion that is based on passive faith; in that, Judaism calls for belief-driven behavior, and the expression of faith through deliberate action. Judaism teaches that the garments of the soul are for us to actualize our potential. The trick is in knowing when the focus needs to be our thoughts, when it is about speech and when it must manifest through action.

So, the next time you face a challenge, decide first whether grounded optimism is appropriate; and if so, try adding a little faith. Know that whatever test you are undergoing is the test you were meant to have, that you can pass it and that you will emerge emotionally stronger, intellectually wiser, and spiritually higher. Become a Jewish Optimist, and there is no telling how many seas you will be able to part in your life.

Internalize & Actualize:

1. Are you more prone to be an optimist or a pessimist? Write down five situations where your gut reaction was either positive or negative before you even knew what the actual outcome would be.

   Optimist or pessimist? Five situations:

   _____

   _____

   _____

2. Based on the above, was your gut reaction accurate? Did the situation unfold as you thought it would? If you were an optimist and it didn't turn out as expected, how did you feel when the result was not positive? If you were a pessimist and the situation came out positively, did you regret the negativity and stress you felt for no reason?

Outcome and reaction:

_____

_____

_____

3. Think about a situation, right now, that you are facing where you are still unsure of the outcome. What do you think will happen? Is that an optimistic response or a pessimistic one? If an optimistic one, are you being an "irrational optimist" or is your optimism grounded? Why? If a pessimistic response, rewrite below an optimistic view you can have of the situation. After you write that, write how this new thought makes you feel.

Situation you are dealing with now:

_____

_____

_____

SOFTENING THE HARDENED HEART

(Yitro/Exodus 18:1 – 20:23)

"The greatest asset you could own is an open heart."

- Nikki Rowe

Choosing What We See

Scene One: You've come off the highway and are stuck at the traffic light at the end of the off-ramp, when a homeless man carrying a bucket of filthy water and a wiper, tries to "wash" your windshield, hustling you for a buck. You silently fume at the pushiness of the hustle, feeling bad if you don't give a homeless guy a buck, but also worried that you're possibly feeding an addiction. You toss him some money without making eye contact and speed off, agitated, but maybe not knowing entirely why.

Scene Two: You're at the same stoplight again, hitting yourself for forgetting to take a different exit, and there he is again. Same homeless man, same filthy bucket, same unwanted intrusion into your personal zone, but this time, something is different - and it's you. This time, instead of seeing him as an annoyance, you see him as a person. You notice his suffering. You wonder how he makes it out there on the street, in the cold, in the rain, for a few dollars. You think well, at least, he's not just begging, after all he's trying to provide a service. You begin to speculate what happened, and what's his story? PTSD vet? Tragic childhood? The economy?

You start to realize how vulnerable you are, and how lucky, that there, but for the grace of God, go you, as you wonder how you would fare if life had thrown you a whole bunch of tragic curveballs. But chances are, the more vulnerable you feel, the more you feel that the capriciousness of life could pull the rug out at any moment. The more you say to yourself, "You know, I could end up on the street someday just like this guy," the more uneasy you will become. And then you have a choice. To quell that anxiety, you will need to go back to objectifying that man. In your mind's eye, he's not every man nor is he any man – he's not a man at all! He's a filthy old beggar who's annoying you. He's a thing. And in so doing, you have just successfully hardened your heart. While this may bring you temporary relief, it will never bring you true joy or happiness, as it does nothing to assuage your existential fears.

In the Torah portion, *Yitro*, where we received the Ten Commandments at Mount Sinai, we were fifty days out of Egypt. Most of you know the story that before the Exodus, every time Pharaoh thought of letting the Jewish people go, either Pharaoh "hardened his heart," or God "hardened his heart" for him, until eventually he had no choice. What does that mean? A hardened heart is a disconnected heart; employing whatever mental tactic it needs in order not to see reality. In fact, the enslavement of the Jews in Egypt began with decrees where the Pharaoh started to refer to the Jewish people as an "it," no longer seeing than as human beings. Once you dehumanize a person or a nation, you can rationalize and justify just about anything.

Scene Three: You're at the stoplight with the same homeless man, once again. This time, instead of hardening your heart, you stay open to an emerging sense of compassion, and your heart softens. You feel good because you feel alive, connected, and present. And now you meet that moment of opportunity with choices. Maybe this time, you offer him a sandwich, or you give him the buck with a sincere smile.

What's in a Name?

The Jewish people had been slaves for generations. The open miracles of the Ten Plagues and the splitting of the sea were completely outside of their experience. In fact, their whole understanding of reality was turned on its head, and from what the Jewish people had just experienced from the plagues to the splitting of the sea, the very laws of nature were up for grabs. Furthermore, it is said that when the Jews stood at the foot of Mt. Sinai, they "saw" thunder and "heard" lighting. They must have been in free fall, going down an epic rabbit hole.

And then, in the only instance of mass revelation in history, every man, woman and child directly heard the voice of God. The first word of the First Commandment is the word: *"Anochi,"* which is an Egyptian word, appearing very rarely in Scripture. It is not the way God introduced Himself to Moses at the Burning Bush when we read for the first time the phrase, "I am that I am." Nor did God use this Egyptian word when He communicated with Abraham or the other Jewish patriarchs. So, what could this seeming anomaly tell us?

It tells us that God gets us and that He meets us where we are. In choosing that first word to be in a language that was familiar, it was comforting. It softened the introduction, so to speak, and thus it was an act of compassion and connection. Despite our increased level of holiness on our way to Mt. Sinai we were imperfect. God saw us in our totality, in all of our human imperfection, and God met us where we were - *"Anochi."* With this one Egyptian word, God joined with us, and in a sense our "worldview" at the time, thereby creating the bond of connection.

God's Compassion

Thus – God's compassion was not based on our "deserving" it. And that is the deep reality of compassion – it is not earned; rather, it is given. It is from this place, then, that we were redeemed. It is from this place that the rest of the commandments flowed. In fact, it is from this place that all of Torah flows.

So, in getting back to our homeless windshield washer; it is not that the homeless man "deserves" our compassion, but that the Divine in us regards him as intrinsically "worthy" of compassion. And so are we all – simply because we are. Says Kristin Neff, author of *Self Compassion,* from which I drew the story and discussion of the homeless man:

"Compassion is not only relevant to those who are blameless victims, but also to those whose suffering stems from failure, personal weakness or bad decisions. You know – the kind that you and I make every day. Compassion involves recognizing our shared human condition, flawed and fragile as it is."[41]

From the beginning, we were created as flawed and imperfect human beings, and without the attribute of mercy, we would not be able to survive. On the other hand, mercy is not without boundaries, limits and common sense. An unbalanced or un-tempered compassion can create harm, and thus, is not compassionate. For example, in the case of the homeless man, it would not be compassionate to enable addiction, nor would it be common sense to bring him home to live with you. And while God starts the Ten Commandments from the place of compassion, the Commandments themselves are about those boundaries and limits that will best nurture connection with God and each other.

But compassion is a good place to start. So, the next time you encounter a flawed human being (like everyone - including yourself), don't immediately harden your heart. Don't default into the place of disconnection and objectification, where you are right (and they are wrong), you are better (and they are worse), you are worthy (and they are not). Try compassion as your first response, and then – from that place – you'll meet that moment of opportunity with good choices, and you will know the right thing to do.

Internalize & Actualize:

1. Write down a situation where you have been unfairly judged and assumptions were made about you without knowing or understanding your situation. How did it make you feel? What do you wish had been said or done instead?

    You were misjudged:

    _____

    _____

    _____

2. Now write down a situation where you have misjudged another and lacked compassion because you felt it was undeserved. If you had been able to be more compassionate with this person, how do you think it would have changed the outcome?

You misjudged:

_____

_____

_____

3. Put together a list of five ways you can practically implement being more compassionate, both to yourself and to others. Make sure to write both what you plan to do and in which situation, so there is accountability. Date this and come back in a few weeks and reflect how that compassion has changed how you feel about yourself and the situation.

Ways to be more compassionate:

_____

_____

_____

WHOLLY LOVE

*(Mishpatim/*Exodus 21:1 – 24:18)*

"How you do anything is how you do everything."

- Anonymous

The Perfect Moment

Sometimes everything aligns to come together in one perfect moment. This morning, my daughter asked me to make her a cup of tea to take to school. I looked in the cabinet. Her favorite brand was right there. *Check.* Her favorite organic sweetener was right there. *Check.* I opened another door to search for a disposable travel cup. Right in front were the cups, with the exact corresponding number of lids, and the exact number of cardboard sleeves that slide over the cup to make it easy to hold. *Check.* I made the tea, looped the string over to the right, and snapped the lid into place aligning the opening just right. Looking at this ready cup of tea, I felt that everything was in order and utterly perfect.

The Perfect Moment - Ruined

A moment later, I heard my daughter gagging and spitting out her breakfast. For the sake of expediency, I had grabbed an unwashed spatula out of the dishwasher to scoop eggs out of the pan, forgetting that I had used that very spatula the previous night to serve salmon. Ok, so even though the perfect moment only lasted a moment, it didn't make it any less perfect. Moments have magic in them, and the mundane is anything but that. When we live only for the high points, the grand gesture, and the peak experience, we miss out on where life happens.

And so, it is with the Torah portion, *"Mishapatim,"* which is sandwiched in between two peak experiences. In the previous Torah portion, *"Yitro,"* we received the Ten Commandments on Mount Sinai. In the following Torah portion, *"Terumah,"* we will read about the building of the holy Tabernacle, the Ark of the Covenant, and the indwelling of God's presence.

Holistic Holiness – It's All One

In between these spiritual high points lies *"Mishpatim,"* which means, "laws," where we read the seemingly mundane laws of damages and compensation for various types of injuries and losses. Commentators explain that "these laws" – which are pretty hard to get excited about – nevertheless are part and parcel of the Ten Commandments, no less worthy, no less holy, no less Divine. In fact, the Torah, which is Divine, cannot be compartmentalized at all, because it is not the nature of divinity or holiness to be stratified, to be "less than," or "more than," "a little," or "a lot."

Because our minds are linear and compartmentalized, however, we need to learn all of the separate parts of Torah, to come to understand its wholeness. Unlike the way we humans view things, Torah doesn't differentiate between any and all areas of life, or between the so-called "worldly realm" and the sacred realm," because these realms are inexorably intertwined and connected. Our days and lives are not divided between "God's time" and "our time," "God's domain" and "our personal space." It is one holistic connection, regardless of our inability to perceive it as so.

In *Mishpatim*, God tells us what "holy" looks like. Act responsibly with people and their possessions. If you hurt someone, make it right. Be exceedingly careful and honest in this world… because our character shows up in how we handle all of the day-to-day things, no matter how small. And while there are many times when we feel especially elevated and close to God, such as the High Holy Days, or the Sabbath or a peak life experience; it is also through the day-to-day seemingly ordinary and routine behaviors that we are just as connected. In a famous poem, William Blake writes:

> *And a heaven in a wild flower,*
> *Hold infinity in the palm of your hand,*
> *And eternity in an hour.*

Infinite holiness lies in doing the right thing or the kind thing, even when unnoticed or appreciated. In the loving comfort of a cup of tea is an eternal heaven. The wholeness that we all seek can be found in a moment of holiness. These moments are magic. You just have to notice them.

Internalize & Actualize:

1. How would you finish these sentence stems?

   If I commit to dealing with people fairly and benevolently...
   If I bring more awareness and presence to my life today...
   If pay more attention to how I deal with people today...
   If I bring five percent more integrity into my life...
   If I remain loyal to the values I believe are right...
   If I am more truthful in my dealings with people today...
   If I bring a higher level of self-esteem to my dealings with people today...

2. Pick the one above that most resonates with you and is most urgent in your life. Now write down five practical ways you can start making the "if" to a "when."

   _____

   _____

   _____

3. We all do numerous kind and positive things for others during that day that often go unnoticed, both to others and perhaps for

ourselves. Recognize the power that each small action has. Write down ten things you can recall from the past week that you did out of goodness for others in your life, including strangers (e.g., you let the person with one thing go ahead of you in line, held the door open, etc.). You will be surprised how many acts of kindness you do. Give yourself the credit you deserve for bringing such holiness into the mundane!

Ten actions out of goodness:

_____

_____

_____

BEING HAPPY – LIVING
FROM ABUNDANCE

(*Terumah*/Exodus 25:1 – 27:19)

*"When we give freely, we feel full and complete; when we withhold,
we feel small, petty, impotent and lacking. We are meant to learn
this great truth; that giving fulfills us, while withholding and
trying to get causes us to feel empty and even more needy."*

- Gina Lake

If you have ever been solicited by a charity, you may have been told outright, or made to feel, that you should "give until it hurts." In the Torah portion, "*Terumah,*" we see how giving is not about "hurting" but about "healing."

In the story line, the Jewish people left Egypt, stood at Mount Sinai, received the Ten Commandments, and then, in one of the worst fits in our history, when we thought Moses was dead, we built a golden calf to be his replacement. After those responsible were punished, God decided that what we needed was a good building project to boost morale. Thus, He commanded us to build the "*Mishkan,*" which is the portable Tabernacle that we carried with us in the desert that housed the tablets of the Ten Commandments.

The building of this Tabernacle, however, required a lot of materials and precious metals. Imagine how challenging this must have been for a slave population suddenly made free, instantaneously going from rags-to-riches, who were now being asked to part with their newly acquired possessions. Unlike any other financial levy that had ever occurred in the ancient world, however, God told Moses to collect these offerings from "every heart-inspired person," thus, leaving it up to the dictates of each person's heart not only how much to donate, but whether to donate at all.

In a way, discretionary giving can be harder. For people accustomed to having no choices, being told to give a fixed amount is probably not too difficult. But what personal experience could the Jewish people draw on to make this type of decision? Perhaps the deeper lesson that God was teaching the Jewish people was that in becoming givers, they would not only become free, but happier as well.

From Slavery to Freedom

In freedom, there isn't always a script or a set formula. It's the sum of your choices that makes you who you are. And unless you have the right to say "No," what is the real value of your "Yes?" A defining moment for the Jewish people—the exercise of giving freely (or not) - allowed them to transition from being a slave to a free-willed human, since the nature of a slave is not to be a giver or a decision-maker.

The Jewish people in the desert responded to this challenge and gave and gave until Moses had to tell them to stop. Their generosity did not necessarily stem from the fact that they suddenly had something to give. It came from a desire to give. Having intimately known what it was like not to have anything, when given the opportunity to make a decision to help, they jumped at the chance. It was a sign of their freedom, but more importantly, a sign of their humanity which slavery had tried to rob them of.

Perhaps it was the intense feeling of closeness and connection that the Jewish people had with God at that time that allowed them to tap into their Godly essence – an inspired heart - which means living from the place of abundance. As Wayne Dyer points out, "Abundance is not something we acquire. It is something we tap into." And that creates joy, because giving in fact makes us happier.

The Joy of Giving

People who give money to charity are vastly more likely than non-givers to say that they are "very happy" with their lives. It's not always about giving money either, as research shows that volunteers are much happier as well. And in a kind of circular fashion, giving not only increases happiness but also happier people give more.[42] It should come as no surprise, then, that *doing* good correlates to *feeling* good. So, doesn't it make sense to be on the lookout for ways to increase your happiness, while you are increasing happiness in the world?

Don't worry – I would never suggest that you become a doormat or give indiscriminately. Giving from the heart doesn't mean that we leave our brains out of the equation. I am suggesting, however, that we take a cue from "*Terumah*" and understand, as Anne Frank famously wrote, "No one has ever become poor from giving."

And now, as you go through your week, notice when you are giving – whether it's writing a check, shoveling snow for an elderly neighbor, giving up a parking spot, throwing a quarter in a stranger's expired meter or providing someone a shoulder to cry on. Make a conscious effort to honor a request from a loved one, give some space and breathing room to a partner, hold back a zinger or find a way to say the right word at the right time. And pay attention to the many gifts and blessings that you receive as well. And in so doing, may you feel more inspired to live from a "heart-inspired place."

Internalize & Actualize:

1. What makes it hard for you to be generous or to let go? If you find you are always giving to others, do you find that you struggle with giving to yourself with that same level of generosity? If so, why?

    _____

    _____

    _____

2. What areas in your life do you find that you feel lack? What would it take for you to shift from a feeling of lack to a feeling of abundance?

_____

_____

_____

3. Write down a person to whom or a situation to which you are able to contribute. What would you need to be able to let go of - whether it's giving up resources, time, a need to control, a need to be right, a need to judge, or a need to look good - to truly help?

_____

_____

_____

20

CLOTHES *DO* MAKE THE MAN

(*Tetzaveh*/Exodus 27:20 – 30:10)

"You must be the person you have never had the courage to be. Gradually, you will discover that you are that person, but until you can see this clearly, you must pretend and invent."

- Paul Coelho

Who doesn't have childhood memories of being forced to wear detestable items of clothing? I still have a visceral memory of an unlined gray wool dress that my mother loved to dress me in, which scratched me with every move of a muscle and felt like sackcloth against my skin. A child's only defense is to grow out of such clothes as quickly as possible or find a way to make sure the garment gets ruined, regardless of the consequences. Then, as we got older, this was reversed and we would fight with our parents over the clothes that we loved to wear – that they hated.

As soon our parents stopped telling us what we could or couldn't wear, society pressured us to "dress for success," although we weren't always sure whose idea of success or image we were even dressing for. Part of this cultural view is the oft-stated idiom: "Clothes make the man."

"*Tetzaveh*" deals almost exclusively with the elaborate clothing and the intricate and ornate vestments that Aaron, the High Priest, wore when he entered the Tabernacle to perform the Temple service. Without this regal and distinctive garb, Aaron could not perform his duties. I can just hear

Aaron's mother yelling, "Aaron, put your priestly robes on already. And don't argue with me. Let's go – God is waiting!"

Is this nothing more than "clothes make the High Priest"? Some commentators state that the vestments were for the Jewish people to recognize the unique and spiritual stature of the High Priest.[43] That view suggests that our teenage angst was justified, and it's all about other peoples' perceptions and external reality. *But that would be a very superficial interpretation.* What if the outer garments we wear affect us on an internal level, which in turn can create a new external reality? So, which is it – external or internal reality?

To Walk a Mile in Someone's Sandals

The Torah describes the vestments as being for the "splendor and glory" of Aaron. You may think that these two words mean the same thing; but they don't. "Glory" refers to our God-given qualities, our inherent strengths, and gifts. "Splendor," on the other hand, refers to what we do with them. There is a saying that our life is a gift to God, but that what we do with our lives is our gift back to God.

In order to make that remotely meaningful, however, we have to understand the exalted essence of a human being. That's a challenge at any time, but put yourself in Aaron's shoes – or sandals – for a moment. One day, he's a subject of Egypt; the next, he's the High Priest serving on behalf of the entire Jewish nation. That's a colossal shift. How could he possibly have felt worthy and up to the task?

Fake It 'Til You Reveal It

We usually think that attitude drives behavior. That makes sense. After all, we see how our actions flow from our beliefs and thoughts. The Torah tells us, however, that the reverse is just as true, if not more so, and Positive Psychology research, such as Daryl Bem's "Self-Perception Theory,"[44] explains that behavior does, in fact, more effectively drive attitude.

This can be consciously manipulated for the good; by engaging in specific practices to shape the belief about one's self, that effort will in turn reinforce the positive behavior. We often hear the phrase "fake it 'til you make it." Judaism tells us to "fake it 'til you become it," and deeper still is the challenge to "fake it 'til you reveal what is already there."

For Aaron to assume his role and serve the Jewish people, he needed to see himself as being worthy, to understand his inherent royal nature. The holy vestments were external vehicles to get to that inner truth. Interestingly, nothing could serve as a barrier – not even so much as a bandage – between Aaron's body and his vestments. This prohibition is meant to teach us that the physical and emotional impediments we place between holiness and ourselves, and between God and us, are foreign objects that don't belong there.

Tapping into Glory

We are all glorious in that each of us has God-given qualities, unique strengths, and talents. But unless we know that they are there, we can't tap into them. Unless we know who we are, we can't comprehend our mission and begin to actualize our potential.

May we all use the lesson of "*Tetzaveh*" to clothe ourselves in new behaviors and new ways of being. And when we remove barriers and impediments to Godly connection, we open the way to a new internal reality sourced in our "glorious" essence; thus, revealing a new external reality where we can create the "splendorous" life that we are meant to live.

Internalize & Actualize:

1. If you could imagine your life as the gift you want to give to God, what would your life look like?

    _____

    _____

    _____

2. Are feelings of unworthiness, or the fear that you're not "up to the task," holding you back in your life; whether in your career, relationship, or personal growth? List a few examples where you feel this way:

   _____

   _____

   _____

3. How can you use the situations above and take a "fake it 'til you reveal it" approach? List five practical ways you can start "acting" in the way you want to become your new truth.

   _____

   _____

   _____

HOW SOLID IS YOUR
SENSE OF SELF?

(*Ki Tisa*/Exodus 30:11 – 34:35)

"It's important to determine which surroundings work best for you,
and then build that environment to suit your needs."

- Marilu Henner

In the aftermath of a scandal having to do with embezzlement from a charity, a woman wrote an article chiding people who responded with moral outrage, suggesting that none of us can be certain of how we would act under similar circumstances, and therefore, we should not be so self-righteous and judgmental. I thought that assertion was ridiculous. I know myself pretty well, and I couldn't imagine any set of factors that would induce me to act like that. Really - embezzling from a charity? No way! And so, my moral outrage stayed intact, thank you very much.

The Torah portion, "*Ki Tisa*," is about the sin of the Golden Calf. I would like to think that I would never have participated in that disastrous spectacle. If you have seen the movie, *The Ten Commandments*, where Charlton Heston calls out, "Whoever is for the Lord, join me!" and a woman's voice cries out from the crowd, "I will!" - I would like to think that I am that kind of girl. I would like to think that in any situation, my highest, best, bravest self would guide me, injecting me with the fortitude to do the right thing, no matter what. But that would be naïve thinking.

Historically, psychologists used to believe that what matters most are the nature and character of the individual, and that "we are who we are," and who we are - for better or worse - doesn't vary, and we don't easily change our spots. Trying to change a character trait, the pundits thought, was as futile an endeavor as trying to be taller, for example, and so little attention was paid to the environment or situation in studying character. In the last few decades, the social sciences offer a different view of the solidity of the self and the infallibility of character. And when you hear the studies, you might get a little uncomfortable.

The Shock "Ouch!"

In a landmark experiment, which shook the psychological world, Yale University psychologist, Stanley Milgram, measured the willingness of study participants to obey an authority figure that was instructing them to commit acts against their personal conscience. He was testing the theory of whether people are inherently evil or situationally evil. Could a so-called "normal person" be induced to commit an immoral act and if so, what would it take?[45]

Test subjects were told that they were participating in a study to understand the effect of physical punishment on memory, in which they were to administer escalating electric shocks for mistakes. They would administer progressively harder memory tests to someone hooked up to a machine that would deliver higher and higher levels of electricity when the person failed to recall a string of words. The person administering the memory test was unaware that he or she was the actual test subject, and thought it was to study the memory of the person in the chair. But it was actually a study of induced cruelty submissive to authority.

At 150 volts, the person would be yelling to be let out of the experiment. At 450 volts, the person would fall silent, presumably dead. In between 150 volts and 450 volts, the person would be begging, crying, convulsing, etc. The machine was fake, the victims were actors, but the results were real and they were "shocking." As the person in the chair would begin to beg and cry for the shocks to stop, the participants would look up to see whether they should keep going. The "authority figure" (who held nothing more threatening than a clipboard) would simply and calmly say, "please continue," or "the experiment must go on." The participants obliged, despite the lack of threat or coercion.

Prior to the study, the prediction was that most people would stop at 150 volts, and that a minute fraction of the test population (one-tenth of a percent, which roughly corresponds to the statistical probability of sociopaths) would administer an electric shock at fatal or near fatal levels. Boy did science get it wrong. A whopping 63% of the participants were willing to administer shocks at near fatal levels! Simply because they were told to.

As a result of this and other experiments (which were repeated in other guises but with similar results), researchers started looking seriously into the effect of groups and external environments on behavior. And so now it is claimed that the greatest predictor of behavior is the situation, the circumstances and the context – hence, the phrase: "situational press."

Perhaps this helps to explain the incident of the Golden Calf. It is simply too easy to dismiss those who participated as being the riff-raff that tagged along with the Jewish people when they left Egypt. It is too easy to look at them as "unworthy," "less than," "and not like us," so that we can keep our moral outrage intact, and assume we are invincible.

The Power of Environment

Our environment influences us a great deal more than we think. Whether we get married, whether we smoke, whether we do a host of things...depends a lot on our social network and the people around us, because "social power" can exceed "will power." Of course, *"Pirkei Avot,"* (a tractate in the Talmud, called Ethics of Our Fathers) said as much when the Rabbis advised that in picking where to live, you should make sure that you have a good neighbor.

But like any force, situational press has its negative and positive applications. Just as there are situations and people who can bring out the worst in you, the reverse is just as true! Once you realize the power of "situational press," you can consciously create the environment, the social network, the physical surroundings, the activities and partners that are healthy, that support and reinforce your goals and aspirations. You can use "situational press" to surround yourself with that which inspires, uplifts and elevates you, rather than that which brings you down and undermines and sabotages your true goals. Understand and use "situational press," or the "power of the situation" to your best advantage so that you can better forge your true identity and shape your own destiny. In so doing, you will create such a solid sense of yourself, that no matter what challenges face you, you know for sure what kind of person you would be, what kind of choices you would make and what you know you will stand for.

Internalize & Actualize:

1. Take an inventory of what you allow into your space, into your head and into your life. Is it conducive to bringing out the best in you? Why or why not?

   _____

   _____

   _____

2. Think of a time when you agreed to do something that afterwards you realized went against your beliefs and values. In thinking back, what made you do it? If faced with the same scenario again, how would you now handle it differently?

   _____

   _____

   _____

3. Most of us have a lot of people we are friendly with; but true friends and mentors are harder to come by. List those who you feel bring out the best in you and have the most positive impact in your life. Then, make a practical plan to have more quality time with those people (arrange a weekly coffee date or phone call, schedule a time to call and ask for advice, etc.). What's your action plan?

   _____

   _____

   _____

LIVING THE DREAM

(*Vayakhel*/Exodus 35:1 – 38:20)

"Where there is no vision, the people perish."

– Proverbs 29:18

When you read the Torah portion, *"Vayakhel,"* you could easily think you are having a déjà vu experience. Much of this Torah portion is a recap of the last three. We just read God's instructions to Moses about building the Tabernacle; now, we are getting the "instant replay" as Moses repeats the same message to the Jewish People. Since we are told that there is no superfluous word in the Torah, what gives?

Previously, the building of the Tabernacle was referred to in the future tense – "And they *shall* make...." Now that it is a fait accompli and the Tabernacle is finished, the language is in the past tense: "And they *made...*" This double rendition is for emphasis; considering how many projects fail to get off the ground, it is no small task to see a dream become a reality.

Building Your Dream House

Imagine building your dream house. You hire an architect to draw up the plans and a contracting firm to actualize them. The number of hours, meetings and conversations that go into the planning stage alone are incalculable. In order to get from a "dream home" to actual living quarters, you need to be very clear and specific.

When I renovated my kitchen, for example, I wanted to have a "bread drawer." In case you don't know what a "bread drawer" is, it's a drawer that is lined in metal with a lid with perforated holes, supposedly to keep bread fresh for a longer period of time. When my gourmet ooh-la-la kitchen was completed and unveiled, I pulled out the designated drawer, saw that it was a regular drawer, and asked with a trace of annoyance: "So where is the bread drawer?" My stunned contractor looked around, grabbed a loaf of bread, threw it in the drawer and said, "There – now you have a bread drawer."

I guess we never clearly had the "bread drawer conversation." Putting thoughts into actual words creates clarity, and it is a step that cannot be overlooked. Looking back, the "bread drawer" thing was absurd. When you are creating a dwelling place for holiness, on the other hand, the details really do matter. God was very specific and clear. For a reason.

Bringing Dreams to Life

Have you ever seen a building project get off the ground? The most important thing to inspire donors is to get an artistic rendering of what the building or site will look like. To create a dream, you need to visualize it. That's how we bring dreams to life. And words themselves help that process, because of a simple but powerful truth – *words create worlds*. God spoke reality into existence, and so do we. We create our own reality with our words.

People who make verbal commitments feel obligated to follow through on their commitments because they fear their own internal cognitive dissonance or external social rejection. No one likes to feel like a fraud, or risk being perceived by others as being a phony.

Understanding this dynamic can help bolster your convictions when you need persistence to follow through. But why is the Torah so repetitive? Perhaps it is this – when we are creating something bold and exciting, something we love and yearn to actualize, we have an endless capacity for detail and repetition. We are not bored by the repetition of things that excite us. To the contrary, repetition increases our joy because it allows us to savor things more fully, and experience greater nuances. For example, how often will you study the finalized blueprints of your dream house? How many hours will you spend anticipating, visualizing, dreaming – and talking - about the finalized project?

Staying Engaged

When you consciously visualize your dream as if you were already living it, and you imagine yourself living and acting from that new place of reality, you are much more likely to bring that reality into being. When you then speak about that dream, it helps bring that reality to the hearts and minds of others as you share your vision with them. And your speech is then one step closer to action as now those thoughts have been given vessels through the words.

Lastly, savor the process and the details, and you are well on your way to making your inner and outer abode the dwelling place of your own dreams. We need to be careful not to bore our friends, but in the privacy of our minds, or when consulting with our "dream team," we should be full-out engaged, even to the point sometimes of being consumed. Adding a good dose of passion to your purpose will fuel your engagement. In the words of the poet, Charles Bukowski, "If something burns your soul with purpose and desire, it's your duty to be reduced to ashes by it. Any other form of existence will be yet another dull book in the library of life." Go ahead. Start dreaming.

Internalize & Actualize:

1. Write down what you dreamt of doing when you were ten years old. What are you doing now? Is there a connection between the two?

    _____

    _____

    _____

2. What dreams do you have now as an adult? Write a few. Then pick the one that you feel you can make a reality. Write five things you can do to start actualizing that dream.

_____

_____

_____

3. Write down how your life will look and what will change when your dream is a reality. Make this your narrative that you can now repeat to yourself and to others in terms of how you visualize your future.

_____

_____

_____

23

BUILDING RELATIONSHIP CAPITAL

(*Pekudei*/Exodus 38:21 – 40:38)

"Constant repetition carries conviction."

- Robert Collier

Rabbi Lord Jonathan Sacks, former Chief Rabbi of the UK, was addressing a room packed with students. "Why is it," he asked the audience, "that there are only thirty-one verses in the Torah to describe the entirety of the act of creation by God, and yet, when it comes to describing the building of the Tabernacle, it goes on and on for hundreds of verses?"

For the last three Torah portions, we have been reading the "blueprints" for building the Tabernacle, and now, in the Torah portion, *Pekudei*, the building process itself is described. Is this necessary? Honestly – it seems redundant and somewhat boring.

Rabbi Sacks explained that it is nothing for God, an Infinite Being, to create a home for man, but it's quite another thing for man to create a home for God – especially when this holy building project followed on heels of the Golden Calf. And the sin of the Golden Calf is especially egregious and puzzling, since it followed revelation of the Ten Commandments at Mt. Sinai.

During revelation, the Jewish People were enveloped in a mass ecstatic experience, and they proclaimed their faithful devotion with these famous words: *"N'aseh v' Nishma,"* meaning, *"we will do and we will hear.*" So deep was their love for God at that moment, that they had no preconditions for accepting Torah. Imagine your beloved asking you to do something for him or her - do you need to know the exact details before consenting?

But the experience was transitory. The Jewish People quickly rose to the occasion, and then, having risen so high, they had nowhere to go but down. It is one thing to be swept up in an ecstatic moment, but it is quite another to maintain it for the long haul.

Any relationship can be sparked by infatuation and it's easy to get caught up in a moment of intense feelings. But for a relationship to endure, one has to relish and savor it, day after day, week after week, etc. In tasking us with the building of the Tabernacle - where we did ordinary tasks repeatedly for a prolonged period of time - God was teaching us a lesson about the real nature of love.

More so, in discussing the Tabernacle, there is an unusual statement. We read of this in the Torah portion, *Shemot*, where it says: "*Asu Li Mikdash, v'shachanti b'tocham*,"[46] meaning, "Make for me a sanctuary, and I will dwell amongst *them*." The obvious question is that this statement appears to be grammatically incorrect. "Sanctuary" is in the singular, and yet "them" is in the plural. On a deeper reading, however, it is the essential point and purpose of why the Tabernacle was to be built in the first place. The commentaries explain that the Tabernacle must be built within each and every one of us. We must create a home that is welcome, open and loving for our Creator. We must make a home for Godliness in our individual lives. For when one feels at home, and in this case when the Holy One feels at home, that is the greatest expression of love.

Another allusion to this is the fact that the Torah begins with the second letter of the Hebrew alphabet, "*beit*," which can also be read as the word "*bayit*" meaning "house." This implies that the very purpose of God's creation of a home for man was for man to then create a dwelling place for God, and a place where others can feel at home as well. To do so requires constant work and focus. To make a house a home we need it to be inviting and welcoming for others, and filled with love and light.

Real love doesn't extinguish after one intense fiery moment, but it burns with an eternal flame. When you love, the seemingly mundane and repetitive moments are anything but, and they add up to a lifetime of deep and meaningful connection. The cup of coffee thoughtfully put on my desk every morning, my smile across the table to my husband that catches his eye and wordlessly speaks love, the small daily constant gestures of thoughtfulness and devotion – these comprise the blueprints of intimacy. It is the very nature of such repetition that lays the foundation of how we build loving lasting relationships, and a fit home for God, indeed. After all, as the saying goes, if you want an important guest to stay at your house, you better provide a comfy chair.

Repetition reminds us of what is important, essential and the underlying reason and purpose for what it is that we are doing in our lives and with our lives. It is when we invest in a relationship so it doesn't sputter out when infatuation fades or crumbles, that the work of relationship begins. And it is the path through which our relationship with God – and with others – can become more real, deeper, more intimate, and over time, evolve into its true relationship potential.

Internalize & Actualize:

1. Think about the mundane moments in your life. What do you possibly take for granted that when reflecting more closely shows you how loved you are? List at least five things that you receive or give in this category.

   _____

   _____

   _____

2. Consider making a mental shift from doing things in a habitual, repetitive and mundane way to investing in your relationship. What new loving behaviors can you do consistently to invest in and grow your relationships? Can you bring a new awareness or mental presence to rote activities? What changes?

   _____

   _____

   _____

3. Is your house a home? Is it a place you feel you and others are totally comfortable? Is it a dwelling place for God? If so, what makes it that way? If not, what can you do to create such an environment?

_____

_____

_____

VAYIKRA
-LEVITICUS-

HEARING THE VOICE OF GOD

(*Vayikra*/Leviticus 1:1 – 5:26)

"To hear the voice of God, you must turn down the volume of the world."

- Holly Taylor

Except for seeing the Harlem Globetrotters when I was a kid (and I'm not sure that counts), I have only been to one professional basketball game in my life. I have, on the other hand, never missed a home game of my daughter's high school basketball team.

Here's what I noticed. In the professional game, when a player from the visiting team was making foul shots, lights flashed throughout the stadium instructing the fans to boo and make a pandemonium to try to distract the player from being able to concentrate. When my daughter's team plays, on the other hand, they know that there is no sportsmanship in trying to throw people off their game, and so when a player from either team is making foul shots, there is dead silence.

We all know that noise is a distraction. Casinos overload you with noise and lights to distract you from the fact that you are losing money and to help you lose track of time. Noise can be manipulative. Stores pipe in music to evoke specific emotions targeted to affect and alter your shopping choices. When noise is negative (as most noise is these days) it is far more destructive than being distracting or manipulative; it blocks us from hearing the positive - thereby distorting reality and stunting potential.

You Have an Incoming Call

The first word of the Torah portion, *"Vayikra,"* literally means, "and He called ..." Who was the caller? God, of course. Who was the listener? Moses. What was going on? God was talking to Moses about the procedures for offering the various sacrifices in the Tabernacle. Moses wasn't having a private audience with God, however. Rashi, the famous medieval commentator, points out that other people were standing around, so why couldn't they also hear the voice of God? Or at least eavesdrop on the conversation?

Despite their physical proximity, they simply weren't spiritually attuned to "God's frequency," and so only Moses was able to hear God's instructions. Apologizing for the analogy, Rabbi Frand, a popular lecturer on the weekly Torah portion, compared it to a dog whistle. While the sound waves emitted from a dog whistle literally land on a human eardrum, unlike a dog, the human ear is not attuned to make sense of that frequency. There is no shame in not being able to hear a dog whistle; after all, we are not meant to hear it. Being able to "hear" the message of Godliness, on the other hand, is our very spiritual mission. *"Shema Yisroel – Hear O' Israel,"* is the Jewish foundational message; hence our spiritual eardrums are designed to pick up God's signal. [47]

Static on the Line

There is so much noise everywhere, so much distortion and interference, that it's hard to pick up a clear signal. What can we do about it? Let's start on a practical level and look at noise reduction in our lives. In one of my favorite go-to books, *Before Happiness*, which is a fantastic instruction manual for creating positive reality, Shawn Achor discusses how noise is more than just a mere distortion, in that it blocks out the very signals that can point towards positive growth. In order to reduce noise, we need to do 3 things:

1. Stop Our Addiction to Noise:

The world is a huge noisemaker. It throws billions and billions of bits of information per second at us. While our senses can receive a lot of that data, the conscious brain, on the other hand, can only process about 40 bits per second. Out of myriads of possibilities, we choose which infinitesimal slice of data we wish to perceive, from which we then construct our versions of reality. Says Achor:

> We can choose either to hear negative, flawed, or irrelevant information or to absorb information that will help us to accomplish our goals. But because the amount we hear is limited, there is a trade-off; the more negative information we take in, the less positive signal we can hear, and vice versa.[48]

We only have a narrow bandwidth to work with. When we listen to gossip and negative judgments, when we glue ourselves to the nightly news, or obsessively check our emails, Facebook, etc., we are using up and cluttering that tiny little bandwidth of reality. If we can only utilize 40 bits per second, what do we really want to use them for? The good news is that studies in positive psychology and neuroscience have demonstrated that even a five percent reduction in noise significantly improves our chances of picking up positive signals.

2. Cancel the Internal Noise:

It's not just the noise that's "out there" that affects you. Have you listened to your own thoughts lately? You know that "voice," the one that wears you down with its constant pessimism, self-doubt and negativity. It's even more harmful than external noise because we don't evaluate or challenge its validity and so the effect of this unchecked internal voice has a greater ability to kill our positive potential. We all know about the concept of a self-fulfilling prophecy. Words create worlds. And words destroy worlds as well. Learning strategies for reducing this internal noise, therefore, is critically important and will result in huge payoffs in all areas of your life. Says Achor, try replacing patterns of negative thinking with these three thoughts:

1. I will keep my worry in proportion to the likelihood of the event.
2. I will not ruin ten thousand days to be right on a handful.
3. I will not equate worrying with being loving or responsible.

3. Recognize the Signal:

"Signal is information that is true and reliable and alerts you to the opportunities, possibilities, and resources that will help you reach your fullest potential."[49] How can we hear the voice of Godliness today, which is trying to help us reach our spiritual potential?

There was a famous incident when Elijah the Prophet encountered an angel in the desert. All of a sudden, a powerful wind shattered the mountains, but the angel said, *"God is not in the wind."* Then there was an earthquake, and the angel said, *"God is not in the earthquake."* Then there was a fire, and again, the angel said, *"God is not in the fire."* What emerged after the fire, however, was a still, thin sound. The echo of God's voice that spoke the world into existence reverberates to this day – if we can hear it. Anger disconnects people, and so they yell to be heard "over the distance." Love, on the other hand, brings us close, so close that the barest whisper is loud enough for us to hear the words of our beloved. The "small thin sound" then, is all around us.

Learn to distinguish between "noise" and "signal." Understand that destructive noise spotlights the negative, obfuscates the positive and kills your potential. Stop the noise, as much as you can. Choose your inner thoughts and quiet your brain. "And He called" means that God called - and is still calling us. It's up to us to tune in to the signal and to listen.

Internalize & Actualize:

1. What external noise do you allow into your head that you can eliminate? Think about the time you spend online, listening to gossip or other unproductive and negative noise that is taking up precious space in your head. List a few things that you can immediately reduce:

   _____

   _____

   _____

2. What internal noise is bringing negativity into your reality? What can you eliminate that will help you stay and feel more positive?

_____

_____

_____

3. When you listen carefully, what healthy and loving messages are being directed to you, either from others or from yourself, that you can pay attention to when you block out the other distracting internal and external noise? What messages do you want to hear that you may have been missing out on? List them below and then try this week to "listen louder" to tap into that signal that is trying to connect.

_____

_____

_____

THE RIGHT OF REPAIR

(Tzav/Leviticus 6:1 – 8:36)

"By repairing our relationship with God, we will repair our relationship with everyone and everything around us."

- Author Unknown

The Joyless Relationship

Oblivious to her surroundings at a crowded boarding area in the Philadelphia airport, the woman seated across from me loudly informed her husband in clear and unmistakable terms exactly what she expected from him. *Your job is to make me happy. Your only job,* she continued, adding a little oomph for emphasis *is to make me happy. It is not my job to make you happy.* Judging by the blank look on her husband face and his utter lack of acknowledgement that she was even speaking to him, I gathered this was not a newsflash. And by the looks of their worn-out elderly faces, I imagined he had heard this directive hundreds of times.

The Guilt-Ridden Relationship

With the hundreds of commandments given to us in the Torah, which seemingly regulate our every move, one could conclude that God's overriding message to the Jewish people could sound like the wife in the airport. *Listen up people. Your job is to make Me happy. Your only job is to make Me happy. It is not My job to make you happy.* One could kinda get that feeling – right? It's not that much of a stretch. But it would be dead wrong.

Previously in the story-line, we committed the sin of the Golden Calf (not good). But then we were forgiven, and we faithfully built the Tabernacle (good), which became the vehicle for the Divine Presence of God to connect with the Jewish people (really good). But now, in the Torah portion, *Tzav*, God is instructing Moses about the sacrificial offerings that the Jewish people will have to bring to atone for their sins – their *future* sins – as in the ones they haven't even yet committed!

What's with the Eternal Rub-in?

Wait a minute. This seems rather dis-affirming, doesn't it? After the Golden Calf, we were just getting back on track with God. Did God have to rub in the fact that making mistakes is inevitable, thus ruining the moment of reunification with this "buzz-kill" from on high? Imagine getting married and before you even check into the hotel on your honeymoon, you have to sit down for a lecture on conflict resolution, fair fighting and how to appease your spouse.

Some Simple Truths

Each and every one of us makes mistakes, and we will continue to make mistakes until we are dead, or lack capacity. Along with free will, making mistakes is simply wired into the very mechanism of creation. Perhaps if Adam had understood that fact, he would not have remained hidden behind a bush and he could have come clean. It is crucial to understand that while we in fact "make" mistakes; we are not the mistake itself. Confusion on that point keeps us stuck in shame. Hence, when confronted with a mistake we lash out and blame others, and therefore we fail to learn from our errors and we cannot grow.

That's not what God wants for us. We need to understand that we can atone for mistakes and we can change our thoughts and behaviors. Thus, in *Tzav*, God lays out the way to deal with mistakes as part of the process of growth and restoring connection, otherwise known as the "right of repair."

For example, marriage expert, John Gottman, often talks about how a key factor in protecting marriages against divorce is for couples to learn the art of the repair attempt, because it stops negativity from escalating, and it corrects a couple from heading off course. In all relationships – and especially the one we have with ourselves – we need a way back in.

The Joyful Relationship

The laws of the sacrifices gave us a way to process and rectify mistakes, to repair and restore our connection with God. And we needed to know that was possible from the very outset, or else we could get lost in self-condemnation, blame and shame. Hyper-focusing on our mistakes and thinking we are beyond repair leads to disconnection and an outward expression of anger that traps us in a downward negativity spiral.

Furthermore, the Hebrew word for sacrifice, "*korban,*" is related to "*karov,*" which means "to draw close." It is specifically after we have messed up and feel so far away that we are given an opportunity to come back to the One who loves us and forgives us. The separation we can feel at times is not that God is far away from us, but that we have removed ourselves from God. The sacrificial offering is the "right of repair" that draws us close once again. The mechanism is already in place.

And that kind of truth, that amazing gift, can't wait to be told. God was telling us something about fundamental human nature and relationships. We needed to understand that we are not perfect and that we will surely make mistakes – but the relationship will endure nevertheless! We need to be able to take risks, to be vulnerable and to be authentic; otherwise, we can become paralyzed by the constraints of the life-crippling syndrome of perfectionism.

The Eternal Relationship

In *Tzav*, God also instructs us to ensure the lighting of an eternal flame. Providing the means to process and metabolize and move through our errors is the vehicle for growth, and it frees us to maintain our connection with that which is eternal – our relationship to God and our inner flame.

What God is telling us, through all these commandments, is that our job – our *only* job – is to connect with God, and in so doing, we will connect with our truest, deepest eternal selves. Appreciating the critical difference between making a mistake and being a mistake and utilizing the "right of repair" will help get us back on track with keeping lit the eternal flame of our soul, and living our life's true mission.

Internalize & Actualize:

1. If you weren't scared of failure and making mistakes, what risks would you take right now in your life?

   _____

   _____

   _____

2. What do you fear will happen if you make mistakes, especially in your relationships? What are you most scared you will lose? When thinking more about it, is this based on any kind of reality? If so, is the relationship really solid to begin with?

   _____

   _____

   _____

3. List a few mistakes that you have made that you felt there was no way of repairing. Now rethink them and recognize that making mistakes is human and unavoidable. Write yourself a message acknowledging that while you made a mistake, you are not a mistake, and forgive yourself. How does telling yourself that you are not your mistake make you feel?

   _____

   _____

   _____

JUDAISM - IT'S NOT TO DIE FOR

(Shemini/Leviticus 9:1 – 11:47)

"When something seems to go wrong, it's invariably part of a larger right."

- Jed McKenna

Making Sense of the Seemingly Senseless

A cherished friend lies in the ICU with a massive brain bleed; his allotted time on this earth is down to the count of hours. In my opinion, the world is a lot better off with my friend in it, and so his shocking imminent and premature death hits very hard. For the umpteenth time, it seems, I engage in that age–old theological enterprise, "theodicy," which, according to scholar James A, Diamond, refers to "the justification of a benevolent God by reconciling His goodness with what appears as injustice and undeserved suffering in the world." I know I'm dating myself, but that Monty Python portrayal of God as a giant foot that comes down from heaven to squash the puny humans below resonates with a lot of people.

Thus, in the Torah portion of *Shemini*, we have one of those Monty Python moments, a Biblical buzz kill, if you will. For several weeks, we have been reading – and re-reading – the intricate details of the building of the *Mishkan*, which was the portable Tabernacle that housed the Ark of the Ten Commandments. Spiritually, the *Mishkan* represented a portal and a tangible connection between man and God. Finally, in an elaborate ritual conducted by Aaron and his two sons, Nadav and Avihu, the *Mishkan* was dedicated with fire-blazing pomp and ceremony. In a sort of private "after-party," the two young men snuck into the Holy of Holies of the *Mishkan*, bringing with them an incense offering, which the Torah described as a "strange fire, which God had not commanded." As before, a fire descended from heaven, but instead of consuming the offering, it consumed Nadav and Avihu instead, killing them on the spot.

One explanation was that they were drunk. Lawyers refer to this as discrediting the victim. After all, one does not enter God's inner chamber in an inebriated state and expect to survive the encounter. Another explanation is that they chose to worship God in an unauthorized manner, making up their own version of divine service. What *chutzpah*!

Even so, a God that metes out the death penalty for spiritual hijinks is rather harsh. Such a view portrays God not just as unloving, but also as the ultimate petty bureaucrat in heaven, elevating form over substance to a ridiculous extreme. Before accepting the Torah, we were wooed with the language of love. Talk about "the morning after!" Did the Jewish people need to be taught such a lesson? The answer is "yes," but not in the way you may think.

Extreme Yearning

In an article entitled, *The Pursuit of the Spiritual Life*,[50] Rabbi Shneur cites Kabbalah (Jewish mysticism) as portraying Nadav and Avihu not as arrogant and undisciplined drunks, but in fact, as two highly spiritually aware and engaged individuals. Accordingly, their deaths arose not as a punishment from God for misbehavior, but rather, a natural consequence of their deep spiritual yearning. Kabbalistically, Rabbi Shneur explains there are two primary drives in the human experience: the drive to be grounded and also the drive, even to the point of extreme yearning, for spiritual experience. Nadav and Avihu's deep longing to experience God was fulfilled, to the point where their physical bodies were extinguished, as if their holiness was subsumed within God.

Thus, Moses consoled Aaron with these words: "This is what God meant when He said: 'Through those near to Me I will sanctify Myself, and be glorified before all the people.' And Aaron was silent."[51] Given the fact that Moses considered the deaths of Nadav and Avihu to be a sanctification of God - and not a desecration to God - I don't understand why there is a need to create the narrative of a human crime and Divine punishment. Perhaps a deeper lesson is that we can have a benevolent, loving God *and* also see that Nadav and Ahivu were righteous and spiritually striving individuals. Sometimes, you can have a "right" and a "right."

For our purposes, however, it can still be a "wrong," in that Nadav and Avihu are not role models for us to emulate. God doesn't want us to die for the sake of Torah; rather we should live for the sake of Torah – fully in this world - albeit grounded and balanced between our physical and spiritual drives. Thus, our soul-driven urges are expressed in this world via those physical acts, which infuse this earthly realm with holiness. The macro becomes the micro and vice versa.

Aaron's "silence" at the news of the death of his sons was neither passive submission nor denial. Rather, he accepted what was – and then made a choice of possibility in the face of the impossible. While his illness is a hard pill to swallow, my friend did not waste his precious remaining time with bitterness and complaints, and he did not disconnect from that which had given his whole life a sense of meaning and purpose.

It is a very hard lesson. Nevertheless, when we can make an internal space that holds within it both suffering *and* a loving God, we may find therein a deeper connection to our Creator, a greater appreciation for blessings, and the motivation to recommit our lives with more fervor and dedication to that which truly counts.

Internalize & Actualize:

1. Think about an incident that made you really struggle with your sense of justice and your faith. How did you come to terms with it or choose to understand it? Ultimately, do you feel it made you stronger or weaker in your belief?

---

2. Think about a situation right now that you are having a hard time coming to terms with. Draw a line down the paper. On the left side write down what is most bothersome to you. Then on the right, write down some meaning or explanation that would make the left side bearable. You don't need to actually feel or believe these yet, but just write them down. On the bottom of the paper, write how those meanings make you feel.

    _____

    _____

    _____

3. Have you ever done something that was not necessarily rational but that you did out of pure passion and emotion? Was it positive or negative? Was the outcome healthy or unhealthy? If you could redo it, would you repeat your actions or handle it differently?

    _____

    _____

    _____

WHEN TRUTH HURTS

(*Tazria*/Leviticus 12:1 – 13:59)

"The words you speak become the house you live in."

- Hafez

There are certain things we are told that we never forget. Think about your childhood. I bet that some insecurity you still have today as an adult is connected to something someone told you in your childhood. It could be a teacher who said you were "stupid" or a sibling or friend who made fun of you and called you "ugly." Words stick. And they become a part of us, which makes it hard to let go. When someone speaks negatively to us or behind our back, it makes us feel alone, unwanted and isolated. Accordingly, the Torah's approach to dealing with people who create negativity with their words is to punish them in a very similar way.

In the Torah portion, "*Tazria*," we read about "*tzara'at*," which is commonly mistranslated as "leprosy." Unlike leprosy, *tzara'at* are spiritual blemishes, and they appear first on one's clothing, the walls of a person's home and, ultimately, on the body. These blemishes are the physical manifestation that correlates to the spiritual state of a person who engages in "*lashon hara*," which is normally understood as derogatory speech about another person. Developing *tzara'at* is a gradual process, and when unmitigated, it leads to a procedure in which the High Priest proclaims the gossipmonger to be "unclean," and expels that person from the community to live alone until cured.

When There's Something Greater Than Truth

Unlike the secular laws of defamation where truth is a defense, the laws of *lashon hara* don't give the gossipmonger that "out." As a matter of fact, there is a presumption that the person is convinced that his or her gossip is true! If, on the other hand, the person was spreading false gossip – slander – then it's an entirely different sin, because we should not misuse the power of speech to lie. After all, truth is a Divine attribute, and we want to emulate divinity.

So how can we be punished for our negative speech – when what we say is *true*? And why is the punishment one of expulsion and isolation? After all, "Sticks and stones can break my bones, but words can never hurt me." According to the Torah, however, not only do our words hurt the person we are talking about, but they hurt the person who is speaking *lashon hara* - as well as the person or people listening to it. It's the perfect trifecta of bad. But is that fair?

We often think that our perceptions and opinions about a situation or person are the "truth," which makes us feel justified and right. We create stories in our head, and then we live in the stories we create, not even knowing the difference between story and "fact." We decide the truth, and anyone who doesn't buy into our stories is also wrong.

Deep down, the source of all conflict lies in the ego's incessant need to be right, and the lengths we go to defend that need. It is this form of the ego that disintegrates relationships, undermines the fabric of society and disconnects us from the oneness and unity we should feel with our fellow and even with the natural world – hence, even our inanimate objects are affected with the blemishes of *tzazar'at*.

The Mind-Body Connection

Today, the focus of wellness is on the mind-body connection. The Torah teaches us the mind-body-*soul* connection. Gossip is only possible when we are ruled by the unhealthy part of our ego, which is rigidly self-absorbed and sees itself as wholly separate from the other person, and therefore unaffected by any pain that is caused.

Such a person is already feeling disconnected from others, from the community, from God and even from him or herself. Therefore, the punishment of expulsion is designed to help the person feel the pain of separateness. Being expelled, cast out, etc., is so painful to a psyche that fears disconnection that it acts as a powerful form of control. We are wired for connection. Our need for love and belonging is one of our highest needs. But when we are driven by our unhealthy ego, we can override our wiring.

In the wilderness, where we lived in a heightened state of holiness, a mind-body-soul connection betrayed or conveyed our true inner state. The outer was an accurate reflection of the inner. What you said behind someone's back became written on your body. We simply couldn't fake our way out – or back in.

When the person truly felt the pain of disconnection and then corrected him or herself – mind, body, and soul – so that the body was visibly healed from its blemishes – then, and only then was that person ready for the process of re-entry into the community.

The Torah is not trying to break us with an elaborate game of "Time Out;" rather, the Torah is teaching us how to stay in the game. It's not just that the person recovers to his or her former state, but that the person should grow to attain a new level of awareness – post-traumatic-growth syndrome!

A society that allows unhealthy egos to run rampant, causing divisiveness and fragmentation, is unhealthy. A holy society, on the other hand, recognizes the deeper understanding that in diminishing others, we also diminish ourselves. True peace is based on wholeness and connection. When we check our unhealthy egos at the door, the gates of harmony open wide.

Internalize & Actualize:

1. Write down something that someone said to you that hurt you greatly. What emotions do you associate with how that statement made you feel? Now, rewrite that statement into something positive and growth-oriented. No matter what the insult was, turn it into something that you can use in a healthy way (*e.g., I was called fat,*

it filled me with shame and embarrassment, but I am going to use it to motivate myself to eat well and exercise so that I feel good about myself and body…).

---

2. Now write down something you said about someone else which should not have been said. How do you think it made that person feel? After saying it, how did it make you feel? Write down what emotions motivated you to say it and if those emotions were healthy or not.

---

3. We know that speech is powerful and helps create our reality. Write down five statements that you want to hear on a daily basis. Then put them in different places in your home on a card (*e.g., "You are worthy." "You are powerful." "You are beautiful." "You have so much to give"*). After one week, write down any changes you noticed after saying these out loud to yourself on a daily basis. Try saying them to others as well and notice their reaction!

THE WAY BACK

(*Metzora*/Leviticus 14:1 – 15:33)

*"How would your life be different if…you walked away from gossip
and verbal defamation? Let today be the day…you speak only the good
you know of other people and encourage others to do the same."*

- Steve Maraboli

Insincere Apologies

"I regret what I did." "I've served my time." "I'm ready to reenter
society." We've all seen those parole hearing scenes in the movies, where
the prisoner is mocking the parole board by uttering the right verbiage,
yet doesn't mean a word of it. In fact, according to Bureau of Justice
Statistics, within five years, three quarters of ex-prisoners are rearrested,
and for some crimes, like drugs or theft, the statistics are even higher.[52]
You don't have to be an expert in criminal justice to conclude that
something is not working.

Sometimes when I've had an argument with someone, and the apology
I get seems insincere and calculated just to make me stop taking, I will
ask what motivated the apology. *So, what exactly are you sorry - for?* While
I know this can drive someone crazy, artificial apologies are a deceptive
stopgap measure that actually deepens the hurt and foments an inevitable
repeat upset. And so the Torah doesn't permit the disingenuous gesture.

Rectifying Speech

The Torah portion, *"Metzora,"* describes the lengthy return process of the *"metzora,"* a person who has been expelled from the Jewish camp for having promulgated gossip. While expulsion can seem like a steep punishment for a wagging tongue, the Torah wants us to understand how gossip and slander can tear apart the fabric of a society. The origin of negative speech originates in the thought-process of judging someone negatively, constructing a "reality" around that judgment and then attempting to rope others into endorsing the construct, and so on. Comedic author, Gail Carriger, quips, "I never gossip. I observe. And then relay my observations to practically everyone." Gossip is a virulent social virus, and so the cure has to be targeted to fight the disease at its deepest level.

In order to return to the camp, the *metzora* was required to bring a sacrifice of pure, clean birds. Thus, the *metzora* was to understand that he had misused the noble gift of speech and had made himself into a bird, which is a creature that incessantly chirps (just think of Twitter and social media).

Another part of the ritual required the *metzora* to bring cedar wood, a plant that grows tall, thus symbolizing haughtiness, and hyssop, a lowly bush, to symbolize humility. The High Priest shaved the *metzora's* head and face, and each part was significant. The head refers to cognitive distortion and an ego that convinced the *metzora* he or she was better than others. Shaving the *metzora's* eyebrows sensitized the *metzora* to see others in a positive light. Shaving the *metzora's* beard was to remind the *metzora* to use his mouth for proper speech.

Another part of the ritual involved anointing the *metzorah* in different parts of the body: the ear (representing how the person hears and interprets reality), the thumb (representing action – how the person will henceforth act in this world), and the big toe (representing how the person will henceforth "walk" in this world).

Responsibility and Reconnection

Each component of a lengthy and complicated ritual was intended to take the *metzora* through the process of feeling the pain of disconnection, and then rebuilding him or her, mind, body, and soul in order to reconnect. It's not punishment, but rather rehabilitation – true rehabilitation, as it is meant to be. As I pointed out in the previous Torah portion, *"Tazria,"* the gossipmonger didn't become a *metzora* overnight – it was a gradual process that was unchecked, and so it culminated in this extreme condition. That's why there had to be an incremental process that was strategic and calculated to address the underlying issues. Otherwise, you get the case of the disingenuous parolee – and that's not good for anyone.

Getting back to the insincere apology, that's why unresolved repetitive conflict ultimately prevents people from reaching their relationship potential. As the saying goes, "what we resist persists." So how can we reconnect with someone with whom anger has disconnected us? Let's apply the Torah's prescription and see how that could look today.

Birds - unconscious speech: This shows up when we turn complaints into criticism. Criticism is a global personal attack, whereas a complaint is about a particular behavior. "I'm upset that you came home late without letting me know because now our dinner is cold," is a complaint. "I can't believe how inconsiderate and selfish you are not to call me," is a criticism. If you've been critical, apologize and separate the criticism out of the complaint and stick to the facts.

Cedar wood and hyssop – humility: Don't be so attached to your position that there is no space for another point of view. If you are fighting to be "right" someone else has to be "wrong," and when this happens in your relationship, it's the relationship that loses. There is no true victory when you fight with your partner about who is right. Most arguments are not between right and wrong anyway, but between a "right" and another "right."

Shaving the head – Change your perception, change your story, change your life: We are all meaning-makers par excellence, but what we don't realize is that we have a lot of choice about it. We make up stories in our head, but then we have to live in the stories we create, and often those stories – which we confuse with *"the facts"* - get in the way of relationship. When you are upset with someone's behavior, ask yourself if there is any other possible explanation or motive other than the negative one you have attributed to that person.

Shaving the eyebrows – appreciating the good: We always find what we're looking for. Make it a practice to focus on what *is working*, what a person is *doing right*, and what there is to be *grateful for*. You can repair arguments when you realize that your focus was narrow and that you excluded the reality of the bigger picture.

Shaving the beard (this goes for ladies too) - *words create reality*: We think we have the right to say whatever we want – as long as it's "true." Before shooting that zinger, ask yourself – *Is it necessary? Is it kind? What result am I hoping to accomplish by saying it?* As the Lubavitcher Rebbe said, "To be kind is more important than to be right." So, if you have said something that you should not have, apologize. Own it. Admit you were wrong. After all, love *does* mean having to say you're sorry.

Internalize & Actualize:

1. We all have someone in our life we struggle with. It could be our boss, our employee or our husband or children. Write down five things that really drive you crazy and you would like to discuss. Then next to each one, write if it is complaint or a criticism. Then rewrite any criticisms into complaints that can be said to this person for a productive outcome.

2. Unfortunately, most of us gossip about others. We might excuse it as truth or just venting, but think about the person about whom you are gossiping, as well as the person to whom you are speaking. How can you work on this to minimize and ideally eradicate it from how you speak to others? Think about the places and

situations where it is most likely to happen and what you can do to avoid continuing this negative and unhealthy habit.

_____

_____

_____

3. Think about anyone to whom you may have apologized recently, but you were disingenuous. You said it either to keep the peace, appease the other or just "do" what you knew you needed to even though it wasn't sincere. What can you now do to clear the air in an honest way? Write down a few practical ideas and then try this week to implement them and work on the relationship with this person.

_____

_____

_____

THE BRAIN GAME

(*Acharei Mot*/Leviticus 16:1 – 18:30)

*"Between stimulus and response there is space. In that space
lies our freedom and power to choose our response.
In our response lies our growth. In our response
lies our growth and freedom."*

- Victor Frankl

The Emotional Brain

I knew I was being targeted, manipulated and controlled – yet I
didn't care. When I turned over the cover of the latest edition of the *Wine
Spectator* and saw "the car," I "knew" I had to have it. I put the word
"knew" in quotes because the part of my brain that made that decision
was not the rational thinking and knowing neocortex part of my brain,
but my unconscious, emotional brain, which responds to its desires. Just
as the advertisers hoped I would, my unconscious brain did the emotional
math and put two and two together. Wine connoisseurs drive this car. I
think of myself as a wine connoisseur; ergo I should buy this car.

I wasn't buying a car as much as I was buying my idea of what this car
represented. The subsequent half-hearted on-line research for info about
the car (the auto manufacturer's own website) was my feeble attempt to
think I was enlisting the rational part of my brain so I could justify a purely

emotional decision. Crashworthy – smash worthy – who cares. Anything short of that car being rated the worst death trap on wheels; I was filling out the loan application at the car dealership.

When It's Personal

Even though a part of me knew I was being used, I just wanted what I wanted, and I put the critical thinking part of me on hold. Being a free human being, however, is to be mindful, present, conscious, and thinking critically. Just as we are not supposed to be slaves to Pharaoh, neither are we meant to be slaves to habit, emotions, and unconscious reactions to Wall Street. God doesn't want us to do things blindly in a knee-jerk way without enlisting the support of our rational faculties. Similarly, God doesn't want us *not* to do something, where we refrain from acting - in the same mindless manner.

The Torah portion, *"Acharei-Mot,"* means "after the death" and it refers to the death of Aaron's two sons, Nadav and Avihu, who had entered into the Holy of Holies without any authority to do so, bringing with them "strange fire," that is, an incense mixture of their choosing. While this action was borne of a genuine desire to connect with and to serve God, their actions were met with instant death. The commentaries explain that while their motivation was to come close to God, their behavior ignored the requirements and directives that God had given them. They acted emotionally, not rationally, and their behavior literally consumed them, resulting in their deaths.

God then instructed Moses to tell his brother, Aaron, not to come unbidden into the Holy of Holies lest he die – *as did his sons.* The question arises – why did God deem it necessary to couple the instruction to Aaron with the death of his sons? Besides being a very painful reminder, wouldn't it have sufficed for Moses simply to have told him not to do it?

One of the classic commentators, Rashi, compares this to a doctor telling a sick person what to do and what to avoid. Face it, how many of us take our doctor's advice seriously? How many of us change our lifestyle and habits even after we weigh in, get the lab results of our elevated cholesterol levels, and admit to our lack of sleep and exercise? On the other hand, if we have a family member who died young from heart disease, or if the doctor were to tell us that unless we avoided doing certain things we will die - just as so and so died – it makes it real and more powerful. Therefore, we are much more likely to take the doctor's advice to heart. Whether we are acting – or refraining from acting – God wants us to use our cognitive functions, as well as our emotional desires, in a harmonious way for our benefit. For Aaron, considering what was at stake, God wanted the warning to make a deep impression, by appealing to both his rational and emotional brain.

Leaving the Egypt Within

Leaving Egypt was not just a physical change in geography. Transitioning from a slave mentality to a free-willed human being that could embody holiness was the real journey, and it's the journey of a lifetime. The message here is not to be enslaved by emotions, desires, and unconscious habitual behaviors. On the other hand, we are not to be detached from our feelings and live in a purely cerebral world. It's a fallacy to think that is even possible, and it's futile to pit these aspects of ourselves against each other as adversaries. Rather, they are an inseparable part of the human condition. The trick, however, is to be conscious, so that they support and enrich each other.

In the last few Torah portions, we learned about the mind/body/soul connection, where improper negative speech, borne of improper thoughts and emotions, manifests as physical aliments on the body. In this Torah portion, we need to understand how emotions drive thoughts and thoughts drive emotions. Be not a slave to either, but integrate them so that you can be in the driver's seat.

Internalize & Actualize:

1. Write down a time where you made an impulse purchase because you told yourself you *needed* it, when it truth you *wanted* it. How did you feel after the fact about the purchase? How did you feel about yourself?

   _____

   _____

   _____

2. Now think of a time that you wanted to be closer to someone or to a situation and yet you ignored all requests/directives made by that person. What happened with that relationship? In hindsight, what could/should have you have done differently?

    _____

    _____

    _____

3. What advice have you been given that you were willing to accept specifically because it was connected to someone you knew? Based on that, what is something you have been through that you could use to inspire others to change in their lives (i.e., to lose weight because it gave you high cholesterol, to quit smoking because you were at risk for lung cancer, etc.):

    _____

    _____

    _____

AUTHENTIC FREEDOM

(Kedoshim/Leviticus 19:1 – 20:27)

"The easiest thing is to hide from the world and its follies, seclude oneself in a room, and be a holy hermit. What the Torah desires, however, is that a person should be part and parcel of 'all the congregation of the children of Israel' --and be holy."

- Rabbi Moshe Alshich

There is a difference between being "free" and having a "free-for-all." Having left Egypt, the Jews were slaves no longer and by definition, were "free." But what does freedom look like? The Egyptian Pharaoh was considered to be a "god." Without the guidance of a higher authority, he could enslave a nation, decree genocide, act outside of all reason, and he answered to no one. In being "free" of all constraints, and governing Egypt with impunity, Pharaoh nevertheless brought widespread death and irreparable damage to his country. This is not the kind of freedom God had in mind for the Jewish people.

A New Paradigm of Freedom

In liberating the Jewish people from slavery, God had to teach us what freedom – real freedom – looks like. Without a paradigm or model to go on, God had to teach us from the ground up. The kind of freedom God wanted us to embrace was a certain kind of freedom, the freedom of being "congruent." Being congruent means that the actions of your outer self are consistent with the values of your inner being. Essentially, it means being authentic and true to yourself.

The question, however, as we can see from the example of Pharaoh who was evil inside and out, is which self are we, and what kind of person do we want to express? Having been slaves in Egypt for over two hundred years, how could the newly-liberated Jew know what his or her real self was? How could a recently freed slave understand his or her potential, much less how to actualize it?

The Hebrew word for Egypt is "*Mitzrayim,*" which means "narrowness" or "constraint." Leaving Egypt for the desert was going from a place of constricted boundaries to a place of no boundaries. To avoid the external chaos of a "free-for-all," as well as the internal panic of being in an inner state of "free-fall," God had to teach us what being a genuinely free human being looks like, and how to create our internal controls. So, the Jews had to learn both "how" to be as well as "what" to be.

One of the main themes of the Torah portion, "*Kedoshim,*" deals with the laws of prohibited relationships. Previously, it was the laws of proper speech - what comes out of your lips. Before that, it was the laws of kosher animals - what goes into your mouth. Laws, laws and more laws. It seems that there is no part of our lives, our relationships, our behaviors, even our bodies, which is not governed by Torah law. That is because Judaism is an inside/outside religion.

So, is this just a new form of slavery? After all, when we were slaves in Egypt, Pharaoh controlled us. In so doing, however, Pharaoh wanted to crush us, to break us down utterly. In total contrast, God desires to build us up, to cultivate our character so that we understand who we truly are – a holy people.

The Freedom to Be Holy

For us to be holy, however, we must be "whole." We must be congruent. We must be holy both inside and out. In governing the multiple aspects of our lives, God's purpose was not to create a new slave mentality, shackling us with a new set of compartmentalized rigid laws to be performed mindlessly, but to teach us that Judaism is a seamless, integrated, and holistic way of being. Therefore, we can't say – "This is for God, but that is not." We can't say, "Before, I was on God's time, but now I am on my time." We can't say, "What I do or say over here matters, but over there it does not." And we certainly can't say, "Well, it's not personal, it's just business…"

And so, whether it's governing what we eat, how we speak, how we conduct business, how we treat others, how we conduct our intimate relationships, etc., it *all* matters. In an integrated and seamless holistic life, everything *has* to matter. And therefore, we can consider that each law that God gives us is another nuance and refinement, another pathway and connection, to help us close the gap between the external being and the internal self that represents our true Godly essence.

When we were delivered from Egypt, we were given the gift of freedom. To stay free, however, is another story. Staying free means embracing freedom as a responsibility to be earned, to be integrated and owned – in other words, being congruent. When we can do that, no one and nothing can ever enslave us again. And that is what freedom – real freedom - actually looks like.

Internalize & Actualize:

1. Can you think of a time in your life where under the guise of using your freedom, you were really just escaping responsibility and having a free-for-all? In hindsight, was it healthy for you? What lessons did you learn and did you find that you ended up creating more boundaries from this sense of freedom?

---

2. What in your life could use some holiness? Think through your thought, speech, action and relationships and write down five things you can implement in those areas to uplift them and yourself.

_____

_____

_____

3. In what ways do you feel enslaved and what are you a slave to in your life? How can you break free from this and how will your life look when you are no longer under its control?

_____

_____

_____

LIGHTEN UP!

(*Emor*/Leviticus 21:1 – 24:23)

"Enlightenment means taking full responsibility for your life."

- William Blake

On any given day, the news reports a story of an indictment for some white-collar crime. I wait for the name of the alleged perpetrator. Not Jewish? I breathe a sigh of relief. Whenever Jews, and especially religious Jews, make the news for fraudulent, criminal or other bad behavior, I cringe and feel sullied in the core of my Jewish collective soul.

Maybe it stems from this week's Torah portion, "*Emor*," where God charges the Jewish people with the task of sanctifying His Name here on earth. One way of doing that is to act in a way that causes people to revere God, which is called a "*Kiddush Hashem*" (sanctification of God's Name). By standing for and becoming living embodiments of holiness, we become God's emissaries, as it were. Sadly, however, the reverse is also true, and when we act in unsavory and hypocritical ways, so as to garner contempt, it is called a "*Chillul Hashem*" (desecration of God's Name).

Standing Up for God – Really?

Sounds like a very tall order – "sanctifying God's Name." Furthermore, we are told: "God's honor is at stake." How is it even possible that we mere mortals can have any effect on an infinite and perfect being? The Jewish people – and the world – had just witnessed the destruction of the most powerful civilization on Earth, along with the toppling (literally) of its many gods. The God that redeemed the Jewish people brought the plagues, turned nature on its head, split the sea, etc. This unimaginable reality was a new paradigm for our understanding of the almighty power of a God who directly intervenes in history. Did God really need the Jewish people to be His PR agent?

Furthermore, this command comes at a time when the Jewish people were barely out of Egypt. Had I been there, I could imagine my reaction: *Seriously? I am supposed to be Your emissary to make You look good? I've been a slave all my life. And as you know, God, I have post-traumatic-stress disorder, my self-esteem is in the pits, and my inner child is wounded to the core. No offense, God, but Your expectations of me are completely unrealistic.* God does not ask the impossible, however. In trusting me with His honor, does God know something about me that I don't know, or am I afraid to know?

Stepping into Greatness

Marianne Williamson famously said the following:

> "Our deepest fear is not that we are inadequate. Our deepest fear is that we are powerful beyond measure. We ask ourselves, 'Who am I to be brilliant, gorgeous, talented, fabulous?' Actually, who are you not to be? You are a child of God. Your playing small does not serve the world. We are all meant to shine, as children do. We were born to make manifest the glory of God that is within us. And as we let our own light shine, we unconsciously give other people permission to do the same."

What Lights You Up?

So, how do we light up? And how do we teach our children to shine? The Torah portion begins thus: "God said to Moses: Say to the *kohanim* (the priests), the sons of Aaron, and tell them...." This phrase is repeated over and over, followed by copious instructions for the priests, who were responsible to properly instruct their own children. Rashi, the medieval commentator, explains that the repetition was for emphasis and thus Moses was "warning" the priests of the importance of this task.

The Hebrew word "to warn" is "*l'hazeer*" and it is related to the word, "*zohar*," which means, "light." Predating by thousands of years a contemporary idea one would find in any spiritual parenting book, the Torah is teaching that the purpose of educating our children is to "light them up from within."[53] It is no coincidence that we use the term "to enlighten" to impart knowledge. True enlightenment is not about acquiring knowledge, however, but about gaining wisdom. Being enlightened is not an external process; rather, it's the revealing of our inner essence and wisdom, our divine truth.

And so, Moses was "warning" the Priests that the process of educating children is not just the external downloading of information but the internal cultivation of their character to reveal their inner greatness, because the essence of parenting is to build a child, and in so doing, to fill the child with light.

Similarly, the essence of the Jewish people is to build this world. All Jews – not just the "*kohanim*" – are charged with being the priests of this world and being a light unto the nations. When we understand who we are at our core, and when our external behavior is congruent with this inner reality, then we could never act in any way other than to sanctify God's Name. And then, being lit up from within, we would shine with holiness, where living in such a way as to honor God's Name, would be effortless and natural.

Internalize and Actualize:

1. We all "talk the talk" in areas where we are not necessarily "walking the walk." Think about a few examples where you may be guilty of this and jot them down. Then, write down some practical ways you can start authentically living what you already believe to be positive and true.

    _____
    _____
    _____

2. Think about a situation you encountered where you were sure you were not the "right" person for the job, but somehow you were the "only" person available or willing to act, and so you did what needed to be done. What did that teach you? What did you learn about yourself and your abilities?

    _____
    _____
    _____

3. What does your enlightened self look like? How is that person different from how you are right now? List five ways you can start becoming more like the enlightened version of yourself.

    _____
    _____
    _____

32

MOUNTAINTOP REALITY - TREKKING TO HOLINESS

(*Behar*/Leviticus 25:1 – 26:2)

"My destination is no longer a place, rather a new way of seeing."

- Marcel Proust

Try as we might, we can't shortchange process. The American psyche cherishes innovation, and we admire the overnight success (wondering why we can't be so lucky). But we usually don't know the back-story. Ask any "overnight success," and he or she will tell you that it was years in the making. As Samuel Goldwyn said, "Give me a couple of years, and I'll make that actress an overnight success."

When we try to shortchange process and leapfrog over a necessary course of development, what happens is that we inevitably fall, and what is worse, we often fall to a point lower than where we even started. When that happens, it can be very destructive to the psyche because we can become cynical and feel hopeless; thinking that we just gave it our very best shot, and alas, failed again. So, why bother?

But wait, you might ask - aren't there instantaneous flashes of insight, moments where we can feel a real paradigm shift in that proverbial "aha moment?" Yes, but these are flashes, and flashes are, by definition, temporary. An "aha moment" is a glimmer of potentiality. It reveals a new possible pathway. We need to create new consistent behaviors to turn that glimmer of a pathway into an actual trail, and in so doing, lock that insight into a new way of being. Otherwise, it disappears almost as fast as it appeared.

The Process of...Process

No matter what, there is a process. We had a 49-day trek that took us from Egypt (Passover) to Mt. Sinai, where we received the Torah (Shavuot). When we left Egypt, the Jewish people were said to be at the 49th level of impurity, and it is one explanation for why the redemption took place when it did; for had we descended one more level, to the 50th level, we would have been considered unredeemable. Every day thereafter that we spent walking away from Egypt and towards Mt. Sinai we ascended one level of holiness, so that when we arrived at Mt. Sinai to receive the Torah we were at the highest level of holiness.

Jewish time is not linear, but cyclical - an upward spiral. "What goes around comes around" is an expression we take literally. Every year, to commemorate that process, we count those same 49 days from Passover to Shavuot, spiritually reliving that journey with the intention that every day brings us higher and closer to the spiritual energy of Shavuot, which is when we are able to receive the Torah and commit to a relationship, a marriage, with God.

Trek Like a Jew

Just as we couldn't jump from Day 1 to Day 49, neither can we reach a destination today without taking the journey. We all know the quote, "The journey of 1,000 miles begins with the first step." When we feel overwhelmed, it's useful to slow things down and remember that all we can do is take one step at a time. And I've come to realize a deeper truth for myself, that the journey of 1,000 miles begins not necessarily with the first step, but with the *thought* of the 1st step. And the *thought* of the next step. And so on. This is a critical distinction.

In every Torah portion since leaving Egypt, God is trying to get us to shift how we think, how we see ourselves, to break down the slave mentality and build us up to being priests unto the nations. All of the laws have an external expression in the world of action, but they should come from an internal reality. "Be holy, for I am Holy," says God. Holiness, however, has to be "whole." Thus, as we see in the Torah portion, *"Behar,"* for example, holiness must permeate our business transactions.

In a free-market society, in a bottom line material world where we are disconnected from holism, many of the laws in *"Behar"* make no sense. Rather, they seem irrational and counter-intuitive. For example, one law dictates that every seven years, all work on the land must cease and the produce that grows is free for the taking. Ask any MBA – this concept is unreal! But that depends on whose version of reality you are buying into. There is an animated musical film that came out years ago – *The Prince of Egypt* – where Moses is feeling pretty down and Yitro (aka Jethro), who is Moses' father-in-law, inspires him with a song about "looking at his life through heaven's eyes."

Think Like a Jew

What is the reality of our lives? What is reality anyway? There is a lot of "reality" out there from which to choose. As a matter of fact, our brains receive billions of bits of information per second, but our brains can only process an infinitesimal amount of it, excluding over 99.9%.

We choose which sliver of "reality" to focus on and what to exclude. Thus, our very perspective is a matter of choice. We can choose to perceive that sliver of reality that will reveal holiness. *"Behar"* means "on the mountain" and it's as if God is saying, "Look at your life from up here. Don't just buy into what you think the world is, what you think nature is, and what you think the reality is. Look at reality through My Eyes. Look at your life through the eyes of heaven."

When I went to law school, we were often told that we weren't there just to learn law, but to learn to "think like lawyers." The purpose of learning Torah is not just to learn Torah laws, but to learn how to "think like a Jew," because everything we do starts in our minds.

Before you take the next step of your journey, remember that it is preceded by a thought. Remember the thought that you are holy and look for that sliver of reality that reveals holiness. When you know that heaven smiles down upon you to light the way, your footstep is bound to be sweet and sure, and you will not fall.

Internalize & Actualize:

1. Write down something you have always wanted to accomplish that just seemed out of reach. Then, write down the very first step that would be required to begin the process. This week, work on doing that first step, and as you begin that step, write down what the next one will be so you know what you will focus on next.

   _____

   _____

   _____

2. What is an 'aha' moment you have had? Did the inspiration last? If not, why do you think it went away and how can you revisit that moment and integrate an approach to make it not just a glimmer but also a trail?

   _____

   _____

   _____

3. Think about something you view in your life as negative. Now, picture that you are looking at that situation from a higher vantage point. What do you see? How can you see it through a holy lens and find potential or even something positive in it?

   _____

   _____

   _____

THE WHISPER OF LOVE

(*Bechukotai*/Leviticus 26:3 – 27:34)

*"Letters engraved in stone are forged in it: the
words are stone and the stone is words."*

- Rabbi Schneur Zalman of Liadi

While it may be true that a rose is a rose, that is not the case with the commandments/laws. In Jewish law, we find that the commandments related to commemorative events are called *"eidot,"* meaning "testimonies." Then there are the commandments that are rational, and truth be told, we most likely would have come up with them had we not been commanded to keep them. Ideally, we don't steal because it is not right, we don't cheat because it is immoral, and we don't kill because it is inhumane. You get the idea. These laws are called *"mishpatim,"* and they cover the gamut of the laws that are needed to maintain a decent and functional society.

And then there is a whole new category of commandments that make absolutely no objective sense. As much as we can try to come up with depth and a reason for doing them, ultimately, we obey because we were commanded to. No one would have come up with the idea not to mix linen and wool (the law of *shatnes*) because it somehow seemed the wrong thing to do. That particular law is just one of many laws that fall into this category. And they are referred to as *"chukim,"* Divine edicts and, like the answer to any child questioning parental authority, we do them because

God said so. And if we don't? Well, that is what is discussed in the Torah portion, *"Bechukotai,"* whose roots is connected to this last group of laws, the *chukim.*

The Fear of the Lord

The Torah portion, *"Bechukotai,"* means "through My laws" (meaning, of course, God's laws) and warns us of the consequences of not keeping His laws, or for performing them, but doing so in a "casual" way. The consequences for casualness are intensely shocking and severe, and by all accounts, they occurred at the time of the destruction of the First Temple. As warnings go, it doesn't get more serious than this. But does the punishment fit the crime?

These warnings were given to us shortly after we left Egypt. And they portended a destruction that didn't occur until hundreds of years later! Since the Torah is timeless, however, then the warnings are as relevant as when they were given in the desert, as relevant as they were when the Temple was destroyed, and are just as relevant today. The history lesson is never over. The question is, when will we learn it?

But how can we learn it if we can't hear it? It's customary for the Torah reader in synagogue to recite these passages in a hushed undertone, sometimes to the point of being barely audible. Imagine how many people would get injured if the big, bold, red-lettered sign that keeps us from getting shocked on an electric fence were reduced to tiny print. Furthermore, at this point in history, the Jewish people were knee-deep in their love affair with God. Like the drug ads that seem so promising until you hear the whispering voice-over, we seemed so happy. So, God, are we in a relationship here? Or are the dancing butterflies and puppies just a farce? If we mess up or just don't do it "right," does it make sense that the consequences are death, destruction and exile?

And if that's the case, then this Torah portion is a real downer. And many people will try to tell you exactly that, because a fear-based and resentful view of God is very prevalent, and is used to justify why they opted out of a relationship with God altogether.

A Deeper Meaning

Chassidic thought reveals a deep insight, however. The word *"bechukotai"* is derived from the word *"chakikah,"* which means "engraving." Unlike writing, which is on the surface of an object and can be erased, engraving sets words into an object, so that the words and the object become one. Understood this way, embedded in the word, *"bechukotai,"* is not so much a "warning," as it is a "plea" - from God to us. *Engrave My laws upon your heart. Let My reality be within you. Let Me become one with you.*

The Closeness of Intimacy

So, why the whisper? When people are in love, they can murmur softly to each other because their hearts are close. The distance between them is small or non-existent, and they can communicate in silence, often with just a look. Conversely, when there is separation, disconnection, whether caused by anger or just casualness and indifference, what happens then? They physically shout at each other, to try to traverse the emotional distance.

Whether we know it or not, God is always near, always close to us. When we engrave Godly reality into our very being, as He entreats us to do, then it is just as impossible to perform the commandments with casualness or indifference, as it is not to perform them at all.

Externally, it is not always easy to see the difference between someone doing something by rote or with genuine inner feelings. That's the difference between something being on the surface and being engraved, between that which is separable and that which is inseparable. "Be holy for I am holy," says God over and over. "Love me with all of your heart." God keeps sending the memo, and whispering the truth, but we have to be close enough to hear it.

Internalize & Actualize:

1. What is something you do, not because it makes any sense to you, but because it is important to someone else? Do you find that doing this makes you feel closer and more connected to that person? Why or why not?

   _____

   _____

   _____

1. Write down three things that are so important to you that they are engraved within you, part and parcel of who you are. Then next to each one, why is it so important to you and what does it mean to you. Are these things bringing you closer to where you want to be and who you want to be? How?

   _____

   _____

   _____

2. God is always whispering to us. Spend five minutes in complete silence. Focus on the sound of your breathing which is an expression of your soul. Then write down what He is whispering to you that you need to hear but sometimes ignore.

   _____

   _____

   _____

BAMIDBAR
-NUMBERS-

BE SMALL BUT STAND TALL
(A JEWISH PARADOX)

(*Bamidbar*/Numbers 1:1 – 4:20)

"True humility is not thinking less of yourself; it is thinking of yourself less."

- C.S. Lewis

The Desert

The Torah portion, *Bamidbar*, which means "in the wilderness" or "in the desert" is always read before the holiday of Shavuot, which is when we received the Torah on Mount Sinai. The classic commentary on this is that the best state in which to receive Torah is when we make of ourselves a desert; meaning, we nullify our egos and enter into a state of total humility.

This makes a lot of sense. After all, the desert is an appropriate place for encounters with the Divine (think Burning Bush) as well as the setting for many spiritual journeys. In the desert, there are no material distractions, no cultural noise, and no exits from its stark reality.

The opening line of the Torah portion is: "And God spoke to Moses in the desert." The word *"midbar"* (desert) and *"dibur"* (speech) share the same root, and so the relationship between the desert and speech – Divine speech – is beautifully correlated. For starters, speech represents freedom. The First Amendment, which guarantees free speech, is considered fundamental and integral to a free society. Slaves, on the other hand, have no voice. They are silenced. Their opinion is irrelevant, as they are not seen as people, but as property.

On Passover, which is the holiday commemorating the exodus from slavery into freedom, we read from the "Hagadda." The word "Hagadda" derives from *"lehagid"* which means, "to tell," and so integral to that transition is the telling of a story, that we re-tell every year. In her TED talk on vulnerability, Brené Bown defines courage as the ability to tell the story of who you are - with your whole heart.[54]

But speech only works when one is able and willing to both talk and listen. And to listen deeply, and actually hear what the other is trying to say, requires patience, focus, and humility. Therefore, the desert is the ideal location for the Jewish people to be open to this Divine speech for there is no distraction.

We don't have to be physically in a desert to consciously strip away the layers of egocentricity that distort our clarity. By shutting out the noise that distracts us, we can transform ourselves into an appropriate desert of open receptivity. As the Lubavitcher Rebbe stated: "Without question, the material world and your everyday needs distract you from living meaningfully." This, idea alone, however, is only half of the picture and we would be missing a great lesson.

The Jewish Paradox

The first line ends with God's command to Moses to take a census. Rashi, the medieval commentator, teaches us to understand this to mean the following: that God loves us and counts us, just like we like to count our prized possessions. We are not counted by ability, wealth or status, but by identity – signaling that we are unique, precious and beloved. No two people are alike, no one can contribute to the world in the same way, and so, we are singularly purposeful.

On one hand, we are elevated, each soul, a precious and unique possession, and yet on the other, we should be lowly, like a barren desert, indistinguishable and insignificant as shifting sand. So, which is right? The Jewish answer is, of course, that *both* are right. It's a Jewish paradox.

In fascinating research done at the Stanford Business School, Jim Collins was able to provide answers as to why some companies are visionary and successful and others are not. The key to sustained success appears to depend on the companies' ability to choose between seemingly contradictory concepts, and the ability to embrace both sides of the coin, adopting a strategy known as the "genius of the *and*" and rejecting thinking characterized as "the tyranny of the *or*."[55] Being limited by either/or thinking isn't good for corporations and it certainly isn't good for people either.

When it comes to receiving the Torah, we must humble ourselves, create the space to take it in and learn, at times, to focus on our collective identity rather than our individual identity. As Marianne Williamson says, "When the ego steps back, the power of God steps forward." But when it comes to living the Torah, we must stand tall and be counted and know who we are. We are created and yearn to reach our highest possibilities. Being a light unto nations and repairing the world is simply not a job for wimps.

The paradox is that we must always be simultaneously embracing both sides of the coin if we are to understand either side of the coin, and that is a lesson, not just in preparation for Shavuot, but for any time of the year.

Internalize & Actualize:

1. Write down five things that take up the majority of your time on a daily basis. Now, write down five things you would do and focus on if you had the time. This week, cut out ten minutes of each day to focus on one of those five. By the end of the week you will have spent more than an hour on something you find meaningful that you had previously not made time for.

_____

_____

_____

2. Think about someone or a situation that silences you, where you feel you had no say or that no one would listen to your opinion. How does that make you feel? Now write down what you want to say to that person or in that situation. Can you think of some practical ways you can begin to get that message across and reclaim your voice?

_____

_____

_____

3. We all struggle with our ego at times. And more often than not, it leads to avoidable problems. Where in your life could you use more humility? What do you think would change if you could lessen your ego?

_____

_____

_____

LIVING FORWARD

*(Nasso/*Numbers 4:21 – 7:89)

"Don't let the fear of losing be greater than the excitement of winning."

- Robert Kiyosaki

Short-term Motivation

When a morbidly obese friend of mine, who was my age, suddenly dropped dead of a heart attack, the shock made me recommit to my diet, and I lost some weight. Less than six months later, however, I had gained it back. While there are exceptions to the rule, when motivation to change stems merely from wanting to avoid a bad outcome, rather than obtaining a good result, the change is usually temporary.

Fearing a theoretical illness, or not wanting to wind up like someone we are close to who hastened his or her death through neglect, can certainly galvanize us into a new mindset. The fear of a possible future bad "what-if" scenario, however, does not provide lasting motivation. What *does* serve the process of long-term change, on the other hand, is flipping the goal into something positive.

If you've ever seen the show, "The Biggest Loser," the contestants talk less about what they don't want and more about what they do want. Whether or not they have been coached to speak this way, they usually won't complain about their fear of dropping dead or feeling sick and tired of being sick and tired. Rather, they will share their desire to be able to play with their children, to walk a child down the aisle, and to be a good role model. They want to feel confident, strong and healthy, and to be able to resume their former activities and physical hobbies.

In the long run, being pulled towards the good serves better than running from the bad. This idea is explained by the Chassidic master, the Maggid of Mezerich, who explains the psalm "stay away from evil and do good" as being, "stay away from evil *by doing* good," meaning that the two are connected. It is when we do something positive that we are naturally removed from the negative.

Similarly, when the "bad" has been internalized, and the motivation to change comes from thoughts such as: "I'm not thin enough, disciplined enough, healthy enough, pretty enough, successful enough, rich enough, popular enough, worthy enough, etc.," then this is coming from a place of lack. Whatever you are, or have – it's just not "enough," and that thought originates in fear and creates the emotion of inner shame. That is toxic to the process of healthy change.

Wellbeing is Whole Being

Shame disconnects us – from others and also from ourselves. Disconnection is the diametric opposite of wholeness, as it is connection that is the very mainspring of well-being. It should be self-evident that we can't use persistent negativity to bring about a desired positive result, but we just keep falling into the trap. No matter how we try, we cannot shame and blame ourselves – or anyone else – into personal growth.

In the Torah portion, *"Nasso,"* which means "single out," Moses is commanded to "single out" and allocate different priestly duties to the descendants of two sub-tribes of the Levites: Gershon and Kehot. The descendants of Gershon were tasked with carrying the accoutrements of the Tabernacle (which housed the Ark), while the descendants of Kehot were entrusted with carrying the Ark itself (as described at the end of *Bamidbar*, the previous Torah portion.)[56]

Not only does the job description itself speak for the different level of sanctity between these two sub-tribes, but the descendants of Kehot are "singled out" before the descendants of Gershon. What's strange about that is that this reverses the birth order, in that the descendants of Gershon, who were the first-born, would be expected to assume the duties that were allocated to the descendants of Kehot.

To serve God, one must "turn away from evil" and "do good." The name Gershon is related to the Hebrew word *"gerushin,"* which means, "to divorce." Thus, the descendants of Gershon were to embody the idea of "turning away from evil" by divorcing oneself from it. Kehot, on the other hand, is derived from *"yikhas"* meaning "will gather," alluding to the idea of gathering and accumulating good deeds – "doing good."

What Do You Want More Than You Don't Want?

So, what does that mean for us today? The lesson of switching the birth order teaches us that at the outset, our initial impetus and motivation to change may very well be sourced in the avoidance of an undesirable outcome or overcoming something negative. I know that I have often been galvanized into action as a reaction to the bad behavior of others. Recoiling from what I *don't* want or whom I *don't* want to emulate has often been a powerful motivator for me.

What the Torah is teaching us, however, is that it is a higher spiritual priority to sustain our growth by being drawn to the good and what we see as positive. For example, if we grew up in a home with strife, we may be motivated not to repeat the patterns of hostility that we witnessed. It's a "good" goal, but it's vague and undefined. It is much more powerful, and much more likely to produce results, when we flip that into the positive, and instead, create for ourselves the goal of creating a home imbued with positivity, loving connections and unconditional positive regard. Then we can take actual concrete steps to bringing that about.

Throughout the Torah, God couples the commandments (even the negative ones) with the words, "Be holy for I am holy." The first of the Ten Commandments opens with the words, "I am the Lord thy God," meaning that every commandment that follows comes from creating a relationship and connection with God. That is because holiness (wholeness) stems from connection – not disconnection – and striving to reach and actualize our highest selves.

I am not suggesting, however, that we only emulate the descendants of Kehot. Both ways are important. In fact, to be *only* one or the other, can be unbalanced and even dangerous when taken to an extreme. The path to growth is a two-lane road – "avoiding evil" and "doing good." The key, however, is to understand this polar duality and to know *when to do what* and how through the doing of good, we can avoid the evil. Tap into either of these energies and consciously choose which will serve you best as you strive to reach your goals and accomplish your mission.

Internalize & Actualize:

1. Think about something you really want to change but no matter how many times you try, you keep failing at it. Now, write the emotions that come to mind when you recall this failure. Next to each emotion, write if it is a positive or negative emotion.

    _____

    _____

    _____

2. Negative emotions paralyze us rather than motivate us, which is why we never make lasting change when those are the feelings connected to that issue. Now, for every negative emotion you wrote above, write a positive emotion that will inspire you to work on this issue again. For example, when one fails at something, one might feel "ashamed." The positive emotion could then be "excited" or "committed," etc. And alongside the positive emotion, write a positive action that you can begin immediately to work on changing this issue.

    _____

    _____

    _____

3. Based on the concept of staying away from the negative by doing the positive, write down five practical ways that when you are tempted to fall back into bad habits or actions, you can do something healthy and uplifting in its place. What action could you do that is positive in place of something negative? For example, if you are trying to lose weight and you are tempted to eat a candy bar, your strategy could be to call a friend, go on a walk, eat an apple, etc.

_____

_____

_____

36

THE POWER OF CO-CREATING REALITY

Beha'alotecha/Numbers 8:1 – 12:16

"The soul of man is the candle of God"

- Proverbs 20:27

"Why is this happening?" I don't know anyone who has not asked that question at some point. And it's usually for something negative. And how often is this question rhetorical? Even if we don't care to admit it, deep down, we know the reason far more than we let on. After all, there is a direct correlation to binge-eating and gaining weight, evading taxes and getting audited or worse, committing adultery and getting divorced, etc. Invariably, however, when the question goes to the deeper issues of life, there is no easy answer, and sometimes, no answer at all.

We Have Total Control

The processes of wrestling with such existential dilemmas vary according to the personalities of the questioner. At one end of the spectrum is an approach such as, "The Law of Attraction." This principle is entirely sourced in self, and so everything that we experience in our lives is the direct result of what we create, generate and attract into our lives from our will as expressed through our energy and "vibes." In a nutshell, this is the operating system of the universe, and it occurs whether or not we are conscious of the mechanism, and even when we get the opposite of what we think we want.

So, for example, when what we want and what we get don't line up, as is often the case, we need to look inside for our self-sabotaging behavior and either clean up our act or uncover what it is we really want. As Wayne Dyer put it so succinctly, "We don't attract what we *want*; we attract what we *are*." Thus, we are the actual creators of all that shows up (or fails to materialize) in our lives.

We Have No Control

A diametrically opposite approach, as evidenced by organizations like Alcoholics Anonymous, Overeater's Anonymous, etc., is that we control nothing. We are simply not in charge. Our "Higher Power" is in charge. And the sooner we admit this lack of power; not only over ourselves, other people, and the universe, the sooner we can be strengthened and guided by whomever or whatever we understand to be running the show. Paradoxically, it's getting the ego out of the way and striving for a state of humble dependence that is the first step towards developing personal power.

Somewhere In-Between

It should be no surprise that Torah teaches a middle path, which is a blend of these two approaches. This third approach teaches that we are neither totally in control nor totally out of control, but that we are empowered – in partnership with God – to co-create reality.

Co-Creating Creation

We see this in the very story of creation. Tradition teaches us that God created the world with all of the potential of vegetation lying beneath the surface. It was not until Adam prayed for rain that the earth was watered, causing all plant life to burst forth. Thus, the involvement of man was necessary for the land's potential to actualize itself.

When God created the living creatures inhabiting the earth, He did so in general categories of species and description: fish, birds, creeping things, wild animals, domesticated animals, etc. There was no specificity and differentiation between the classes of species. It was Adam who named them all.

In the Hebrew language, a name is not arbitrary; it goes to the essence of the thing. And so, Adam saw the unique nature and potential of each type of creature. He lifted out each creature from an indistinguishable mass and raised it to a being with a unique identity and purpose. God spoke, and all of the earth's inhabitants came into existence. Adam, however, provided the finishing touch. Just as the very process of creation is said to be ongoing, so is our involvement in co-creating it. We are God's very partners in the ongoing process of creation. So, what are we creating?

Being a Lamplighter

Fast forward to the Torah portion, *"Beha'alotecha,"* which starts with the command for Aaron to kindle the lights of the Menorah. What menorah? There was no Judaica store nearby and no on-line shopping. Furthermore, the description was daunting – it was to be made of one piece of pure gold, consisting of seven branches with each branch looking like an almond tree - with buds, blossoms, and flowers. Unable to create that on his own, tradition teaches us that Moses threw the gold into a fire, and the Menorah emerged, fashioned, as you will, by the Hand of God. And so here, it was man who initiated an act of creation, but it was God who finished it.

But then Aaron was commanded to "raise light in the lamps." He not only participated in the creation, but it was now his responsibility to ensure that it was ignited to illuminate the greater surroundings. And through being that Lamplighter, that light could then continue to light others without being diminished. Jewish philosophy teaches that the soul is compared to the flame. Once lit, it will both give off light and be able to ignite others. That is what it means to both be inspired and to inspire. But the same way light can bring about more light; darkness has the power to do the same. Therefore, the same process of casting gold into a fire can create a Menorah or a Golden Calf.

As partners in creation, there is an on-going dance between the Divine and us. As "creat*ed* beings," we depend on God for our very existence. As "creat*ive* beings," on the other hand, we can create heaven or hell. Erica Jong quipped, "Take your life in your own hands, and what happens? A terrible thing; no one to blame."

Thus, it is the paradox of the middle path that embraces both realities. We are created with infinite potential. Moment by moment, each choice is an act of casting gold into the fire. What is it that we are hoping to materialize, to create, to become? What do we want to emerge? A Menorah or a Golden Calf?

Says Rabbi Shalom Dov Ber Schneersohn, "The Lamplighter walks the streets carrying a flame at the end of a pole. He knows that the flame is not his. And he goes from lamp to lamp to set them alight." What lamps are we lighting and do they emit the light we wish to see?

Internalize & Actualize:

1. When faced with a negative situation, are you more likely to feel that you are the cause of it, that you have no control over it or a combination of the two? Think of a situation that is difficult for you and then write out how you can find that balance between letting go of full responsibility, while simultaneously exploring what you can do to alter the impact or change the situation.

   _____

   _____

   _____

2. There is the concept that we are all empowered to be "Lamplighters," which is the ability to help spark another's innate talent and ability. Think about who have been the Lamplighters in your life. Write down the qualities they had that inspired you and in what way they had an impact on your life.

   _____

   _____

   _____

3. Now, write down a list of those for whom you have been a Lamplighter. What qualities of yours helped ignite and inspire them? Write down these qualities on note cards and place them around your house. When you are feeling negative, read them aloud, reminding yourself of your strengths and abilities and how they have helped the lives of others.

_____

_____

_____

FIVE STEPS TO BETTER
RELATIONSHIPS

(*Shelach*/Numbers 13:1 – 15:41)

"In youth, one learns to talk; in maturity, one learns to be silent.
This is man's problem: that he learns to talk before he learns to be silent."

- Rabbi Nachman of Breslov

But...

Have you ever been on the wrong end of an unwanted question, such as, "Will you marry me?" Or, "Will you be my date for the prom?" Or something less serious, such as, "Hey, can you do me a huge favor?" If the answer is "No," there is going to be a "but" somewhere in that sentence, such as, "I really love you – but – I'm just not in love with you." Or, "You're such a great guy – but – I'm already going with Mr. Wrong." Or, "I'd love to help you out, but I think I have to do my colonoscopy prep that night."

And no matter how nice or apologetic or convincing the first part of the sentence is, for the listener, it's only what comes after the "but" that matters, because that's where the truth of the message lies. And so, it's hard to believe, but this one innocuous word, "but," is responsible for the downfall of the generation that left Egypt and it caused them to be condemned to die in the desert.

If you don't know the story, the Jewish people had just left Mount Sinai after receiving the Ten Commandments and were poised to enter what was then known as the Land of the Canaanites. The people were nervous and didn't know what they were up against, and so they asked Moses to appoint a group of men to go spy out the land.

After forty days, the spies returned and issued a glowing report. "It's a land filled with milk and honey. Here are its fruits." And then they said the word "*efes*" (which means "but") after which they painted such a negative picture of the land, that people were scared stiff and wept through the night, thus sealing their fate, such that not only would they not enter the land, but future calamities (such as the destruction of the First and Second Temples) would occur on the anniversary of that date.

The Weight of Criticism

We often mix compliments with criticisms and wonder why the listener is offended. I gave my son a compliment about his appearance, but I ended the sentence with criticism. "Mother giveth and Mother taketh away," he said. And I was surprised. After all, I said something nice – *also* – so why the drama? Plain and simple, it's what follows the "but" that counts. And we can't neutralize or offset a criticism with a compliment. It's not an even wash. Evolutionists will explain that we are wired to focus on negativity because the negative carries valuable information about possible danger.

Whatever the reason, a ratio of 1:1 (compliment/criticism) will destroy the quality of your relationships as surely as it destroyed that generation of the Jewish people. So, can we ever criticize? Of course, we can, and sometimes we must, but there are ways to do it without harming the relationship.

In a business setting, there is something called the "*Losada* Principle,"[57] which tells us that unless a negative or critical remark is offset by at least three positive comments, the work environment is considered toxic, and employees will not thrive and be productive. In personal relationships, the ratio is a bit higher. A critical or negative comment needs to be offset with three to five positive comments. Referred to as the "magic ratio" by relationship expert, John Gottman, he warns that when couples dip consistently below that ratio, they are statistically headed for a divorce.[58] Furthermore, a critical nature is more a reflection of the speaker than the object of the reproach. "When we judge or criticize another person, it says nothing about that person; it merely says something about our own need to be critical."[59]

So, here's my advice:

1. If you must say something critical (and sometimes you must) make an effort to offset the statement with multiple positive remarks.

2. If you must say two contradictory things, switch the order so that the nice comment follows the "but." For example: "You did a great job cleaning your room, but the bathroom is a mess" – versus - "The bathroom is a mess, but you did a great job cleaning your room." Do you hear the difference?

3. After you get the hang of that, try to stop talking after the compliment. "You did a great job cleaning your room." Full stop. The bathroom is another conversation for another time. Don't ruin the compliment.

4. Don't ruin the compliments you receive, either. When I got a compliment about a meal I prepared, for example, I often would deflect it with a "but," such as, "Thanks, but the chicken was too dry." Don't diminish yourself and make the person who gave you a compliment feel silly for doing so.

5. And finally, use the "but" in a way that transforms it from "destructive" to "constructive." For example, "I hear that your teacher is a demanding perfectionist, but it's going to make you up your game." Or, "I don't know right now how I can deal with this, but I know it's going to make me stronger." Use the "but" to focus on the positive aspect of a challenging situation.

If only the spies could have read this blog, Jewish history could have been completely different! Let us not make the same mistake in our lives, and instead, pay attention to the many "buts" in our lives and infuse our relationships with conscious kindness and a legacy of positivity.

Internalize & Actualize:

1. Think about a recent argument you had. What could you have said differently that would have changed the outcome of that interaction? What can you say now to help rectify it?

    _____

    _____

    _____

2. Think about someone you are likely to criticize. Now write down five positive attributes or compliments you could give that person that would be sincere. This week say one of those compliments daily and then write down any changes you notice from that person.

    _____

    _____

    _____

3. The way we talk to ourselves is just as critical as the way we talk to other people. Using the three to five compliments per criticism ratio, write down something negative you often think or say to yourself. Following that, write down three to five compliments you can give yourself (without a "but") to help offset the damage from that negative statement.

    _____

    _____

    _____

THE POWER OF THE QUESTION

(*Korach*/Numbers 16:1 – 18:32)

*"And for the child who does not know how to
ask, you must teach him how..."*

- Passover Haggadah

Power Struggles

The Torah portion, *"Korach,"* is the name of one of the most famous attempted power-grabbers in Jewish history. In the story line, the priestly honors and appointments were doled out long ago to Moses and his brother Aaron. Korach, their cousin, was left out of this honor society and was resentful. However, Moses was untouchable as a leader, and so Korach kept his bitterness to himself.

Times had changed, however. After the incident with the spies in the previous Torah portion of *"Shelach,"* when the people knew they were not going into the land of Israel but were condemned to die in the desert, it was a time of crisis and unrest. Moses' ratings were down, thus giving Korach the perfect opportunity to capitalize on the situation and to try to usurp Moses' position as leader.

And Korach did so by posing a simple question: "The entire community is holy, and God is within them; why do you raise yourselves over the congregation of God?"[60] That doesn't sound too bad – does it? Korach was saying, in effect: "If we're all holy, then what makes you guys so special? I'm every bit as exceptional as you." Korach even got a few hundred guys to agree with him because his platform was essentially that he was the champion for the masses, he stood for the little guy, and everyone is equal – perhaps the first Jewish communist.

But Korach wasn't looking to make everyone the same. He wasn't looking to make this an equal opportunity procedure. This wasn't the Biblical version of: "I'm holy. You're holy. And that's OK." Korach wanted to be the High Priest, and assuming he could overthrow Moshe and appoint himself, by the time his groupies figured out that nothing changed for them, well, you know what happens in takeovers.

Selective Questioning

As fascinating as the story line is (and to find out what happened to Korach, read "The Book,") what interests me is the use of the question. When Korach asked, "What makes you holier than me?" it wasn't an honest inquiry at all. He was looking to find fault with Moses, and he was trying to get others to join in, to see reality his way, and he did it through the use of questions, because – and this is important to understand – the reality that we see depends on the questions that we ask.

Isidore Rabi, winner of a Nobel Prize in physics, was once asked why he became a scientist. He replied, "My mother made me a scientist without even knowing it. Every other child would come home from school and be asked, 'What did you learn today?' But my mother wanted to know something else. 'Izzy,' she always used to say, 'did you ask a good question today?' That made the difference."

Let's look at relationships. In the infatuation or romantic phase of a relationship, the part of the brain associated with critical thinking is dysfunctional. When that part of our brain comes back on-line, and critical thinking resumes, we start asking ourselves: "What's wrong with my spouse? What's wrong here? What happened to the person I married, etc.?"

And when we turn these questions inward, we create inner shame. The brain doesn't like unanswered questions and so when we ask a negative question, such as, "What's wrong with me?" the brain will only supply a negative answer" "I'm such a loser, mess, etc."

And while we mustn't turn a blind eye to problems, the tendency to focus *only* on the problems - to allot our entire 60-bit sliver of reality to the negative - shuts out all of the good and wonderful aspects of a relationship. It's as if we are wearing blinders, and if we can't see it, then these things don't exist, even if they are right in front of us. Incidentally, I think this is one of the main reasons relationships fail or suffer, because we become very good at being faultfinders, and we lose the ability to see the good.

Changing What We See

Therefore, if the questions we ask create the reality we see, it stands to reason that we can change our reality by asking better questions. When you change your question, you change what you are looking for. By understanding this dynamic, you can engineer a more positive life and relationships.

Chassidic thought teaches that there is a seed of greatness in every moment and a spark of holiness in everything – how much more so in people? Try looking for the good with positive questions: "What is working? What is going well? What is there to be grateful for? When are things good and what factors tend to make that happen? What's my role in that? What do I do well and how can I do more of that? What are the blessings in this situation? How is this situation calling for me to serve, to act, to change, to grow?"

Here's the secret, and it's a phrase well worn into me by Positive Psychology expert, Tal Ben-Shahar: "When we see the good, the good appreciates." And we see the good by asking good questions. When Korach looked at Moses, all he could ask was why was he not getting what he wanted, why others were being elevated over him, and why was he being denied what he thought was coming to him. In a situation flowing with lemonade, all Korach could taste was bitter lemons. Let us not make the same mistake. Let us look for the good, see the good, and enjoy the many blessings in our lives.

Internalize & Actualize:

1. We all have someone in our lives that makes us jealous. Think about that person and then write down the questions that pop into your mind (i.e., why her and not me?). Now, take those very same questions and change them around to focus on positive growth and development for yourself.

   _____

   _____

   _____

2. Think about a question you have asked yourself, or another, that had a transformative effect on who you are today. Write about the question or answer that made such an impact?

   _____

   _____

   _____

3. Being able to question another or our situation takes a lot of strength. What questions do you have for yourself that perhaps you have been avoiding asking? Write down three questions that you may not yet have the answers for but can begin to work on.

   _____

   _____

   _____

FINDING MEANING IN MYSTERY

(*Chukat*/Numbers 19:1 – 22:1)

*"The best teachers are those who show you where
to look but don't tell you what to see."*

- Alexandra K. Trenfor

Forty-two is the number of stops we had during our forty years in the desert, with some stops lasting a few days, and some for years. It is said that each of us also has forty-two stops in the journey of our lives. After my Bat Mitzvah, and obligatory party feted by champagne and my family's business friends, I was released at last from the obligation of having anything more to do with Judaism. And so, my Jewish journey had a real stop, that lasted for the next 25 years.

The Wake-up Call

Fast forward to my mid-thirties, and I was at a "duty funeral" for the wife of someone my fiancé knew. I could not have anticipated that the death of a stranger would be a life-changing event for me. Hearing how active and vital this woman was in the Jewish community and feeling alarmed over the impact and void left by her death, my heart awakened and, much to my surprise, I felt I wanted to make a difference.

But how? Until that moment, I didn't even identify as Jewish, much

167

less being part of a community. And so, I started on my spiritual journey again, making a series of stops here and there, looking for my Jewish identity and yearning for connection.

For a while, my journey took me to a synagogue, which had an unusual custom. The rabbi's sermon was interactive and participatory. Once again, I could not have anticipated how a rabbi's sermon would have a life-altering effect, but it did, and the sermon in question happened to be the Torah portion, "*Chukat*," otherwise known as the "Red Heifer."

The command to find a perfect and completely red cow, without a single white hair on its body (try to find one), sacrifice it and use its ashes for ritual purification are incomprehensible and irrational, in that the same ritual results in opposite effects – it causes both purification *and* contamination.

Upon hearing this, a man stood up and said, angrily, "What is this, Nazi Germany, that we just have to follow blindly orders that make no sense?" I looked around at the heads nodding in agreement and a silent rabbi. Before I even knew what I was doing, I was on my feet protesting the comparison of God to Hitler and the laws of the Torah to the laws of Nuremberg. The rabbi sincerely thanked me for my "God-oriented comment" and I sat down, my face flush and tears oddly in my eyes.

If one's agenda is to conclude that Torah is arcane, obsolete and without relevance or purpose and if you want to view those who live a Torah–observant life as blindly following irrational orders, then this Torah portion, *Chukat*, fits the bill.

People tend to think that Torah laws come in two categories – rational and irrational, laws that make sense and are good to live by – and everything else. Once we determine that something is "irrational," we so-called "rational beings" feel free – obligated, even – to discard it and dismiss anyone who takes it seriously.

An Inconvenient Truth

But the problem with that much "certainty" is that it closes off exploration, and it shuts off possibility. You have come to the end of the line of inquiry, and you are also intellectually dishonest because you are selective with irrationality.

Where is this so-called world of "reason" to be found? Anyone who thinks we don't live in an irrational world has not had to apply for a driver's permit in Pennsylvania or had to try a legal case in Rhode Island, (where the courts shut down every week because there are insufficient sheriffs to unlock the courtrooms), or had to deal with divorce clients.

And if I were a truly rational person, I would never eat foods that I know are bad for me. I would never use negativity to try to create positive change, and I wouldn't bother taking off glasses that weigh two ounces before I weighed myself. But I live an irrational life. We all do, and we just have to accept that quality in ourselves.

However, the laws of the Red Heifer and many laws for which we see no rational basis, are *not* irrational. They are, rather, "supra-rational," meaning that they are *outside* of rationality. It's just not "figureoutable" and your attitude to that unavoidable gap between you and the unknowable is a good indicator of where you are in your faith and relationship with God.

And so, if you want an example of the ability to live with the mystery of the supra-rational, and to find deep meaning and fulfillment in the encounter with another realm, then this Torah portion, *Chukat*, is also the Torah portion that fits that bill as well.

The Covered and the Uncovered

Fast-forward my life another 20 years and many more stops, to an Orthodox wedding. On the chair was a pamphlet explaining the different parts of the ceremony for people who may be unfamiliar with the customs of Orthodox weddings. The "*bedecken,*" which takes place right before the wedding ceremony, is that moving moment when the groom enters the room, looks at his bride and then covers her face with a veil. With this simple gesture, the groom is making this profound promise: *I will cherish and respect not only the "you" that is revealed to me, but also that about you, which is "covered" from me. As I bond with you in marriage, I am committed to all of you - all of the time.*

And I joyfully realized that this, at last, was the answer to the man who compared God to the Nazis. When we, the Jewish people, stood at

Mt. Sinai and accepted Torah, we became eternally betrothed to God, to the parts of God that are revealed, as well as to the parts of God that are covered – to all of the parts of God - all of the time.

That is the basis of genuine commitment, because *no* relationship, however profound and intimate, can fully uncover or completely unmask another. We contain unmapped territories, hidden even from ourselves. How much more so with God?

And when we accept that, then the very questions we ask change. We don't have to be churlish and demand instant answers to everything, especially since answers can trivialize serious issues and are far from soul satisfying.

There will always be times when you are frustrated, afraid or uncertain when the answers you seek are covered and unrevealed to you, when life seems irrational or supra-rational. When that happens, resist the temptation to fall into an easy and false dogmatic certainty that cuts off possibility and which stops your journey to growth.

Embrace the struggle that is part of a nuanced and complex life. Be humble and stay open to the lesson. As the poet, Rilke said, "Have patience with everything that remains unsolved in your heart.... *Live* in the question." May we all be poets in our soul, find meaning in living with and within mystery, and keep our journeys going!

Internalize & Actualize:

1. We all encounter situations that we can't understand. Think about something you have been asked to do that doesn't make any sense to you, and then write down what positive lessons you can learn from doing something that you may not understand, yet is important to someone or something else.

   _____

   _____

   _____

2. Now think about your own needs. What is something you ask of someone else that may not make rational sense, but which makes a difference to you? How does it make you feel when someone

complies with this request even though it is not something this person would think to do on his or her own?

_____

_____

_____

3. Everyone in our lives knows us in a different way. Some of our characteristics are more revealed, and some very concealed - sometimes even from ourselves. Write down five things about yourself that few, if any, know. How do you think people would react if they knew these parts of you?

_____

_____

_____

40

THREE WAYS TO TRANSFORM CURSES INTO BLESSINGS

(*Balak*/Numbers 22:2 – 25:9)

"Love covers up all iniquity."

- Proverbs 10:1

From a Curse to a Blessing

"How goodly are thy tents O Jacob, thy dwellings, O Israel." "*Ma tovu ohalecha Yaakov mishk'notecha Yisroel.*"[61] This verse, which is this week's Torah portion, *Balak*, is said upon entering a synagogue, is part of the daily Morning Prayer, and even if you don't recite it, you may know it, as it is one of the most famous verses in the Torah.

And so, one would think that these words of praise were uttered by God, or by Moses, or at least by someone "very holy." And yet, these words emanated from the mouth of a notorious Jew hater, Bilaam, who was hired by Balak, (the newly-appointed King of Moab), to curse the Jewish people in the desert.

Three times, Bilaam tried to curse the Jewish people, and yet each time, he blessed them instead. Prior to the first two attempts, Bilaam and God had a "conversation" whereby God either instructed Bilaam what to say or put the words directly into his mouth. Despite his pure hatred and single-minded intention to cause harm, Bilaam could only utter words of blessing and praise for the Jewish people.

Therefore, before the third and final attempt, Bilaam decided to take a different tact, since these "conversations" with God were not going his way. This time, Bilaam concentrated on the so-called faults and transgressions of the Jewish people, trying to discredit them so as to overcome God's benevolence and whip up a host of spiritual negativity against the Jewish people.

A Godly Lens

And so, after he was all fired up, Bilaam lifted his eyes to blast the Jewish people once and for all with his "evil eye." But when he raised his eyes and looked – truly looked – Bilaam noticed how the placement of the tents was designed for the utmost respect for privacy and dignity. He saw orderliness. He saw righteousness. He saw goodness. And he was moved. Incredibly, the Torah states, "He changed his mind to be like God." And in so doing - even if it was a very temporary shift - Bilaam saw a new reality, a Godly reality, and his curses were transformed into blessings.

So, the question is, how could such words of praise come out of Bilaam's mouth and of his own accord? It's true but a not-funny joke, that if a notorious anti-Semite says something nice about the Jews – then it *must* be true. It's just human nature – we have a hard time believing certain ideas when they originate from sources very close to us. After all, how credible is it when we sing our own praises? Thus, if a gentile praises the Jewish people, that's good, but if a Jew-hater genuinely and effusively praises us? Wow – what could be better?

Loving Ourselves

Now, let's take a deeper look and find a lesson we can apply to our lives. Besides our tendency to discount positivity from close sources, I think that most of us have a hard time being kind and benevolent to ourselves. When is the last time you checked in on the inner dialogue in your head and your running thoughts and feelings – about you? I decided to pay attention to my inner voice the other day, and I was shocked at how intolerant and cruel I can be to myself.

Many of us have a hard time liking ourselves. We think it's selfish and egotistical. But if I don't like myself - why should you like me? If I don't value or love myself - why should you? We are also afraid that if we have self-compassion or like ourselves, we would never change, because we mistakenly think shame is the best impetus for growth. And so, we can become our own Bilaams – in effect, cursing ourselves. I can assure you, however, with 100% certainty, that shame and blame are never the paths to sustained change or growth. Ok, you may ask, so what is?

When Bilaam decided to "change his mind to be like God," that's when the transformation happened. That's when the curses turned to blessings. I believe that's the key. In our Morning Prayers, we acknowledge that the soul God placed in us is pure. Further, we are made in the image of God, and we have Godly souls. When we don't judge ourselves favorably, we are insulting our Creator!

Seeing is Believing

Ponder this. The more I love myself - my real self, my Godly self – and the more order, righteousness and good that I see when I look inside, the more I will naturally align my actions to be congruent with that vision. So, may I suggest the following:

Step One: Notice the toxic inner talk. But please don't criticize the inner critic or you'll stay in the same loop. Have compassion and understand that it's a habituated form of thinking. Don't get hooked – it's not you. Rather, it is a bad and unconscious habit, and increasing your awareness of this bad habit will help you break it.

Step Two: Counteract the negativity with positivity – lots of it. In *Shelach* (Chapter 37), I wrote about the Losada Principle and the Gottman Relationship Ratios. In a nutshell, we weigh negativity more than positivity, and so to maintain loving and benevolent and thriving relationships, we *must* offset critical or negative comments with three to five positive ones, or suffer the consequences. I never realized that it applies to our own self-talk as well! And so, every time you hear yourself making a negative comment to yourself, offset it with three to five positive comments that are constructive.

Step Three: Give yourself permission to see yourself with Godly reality. As Marianne Williamson says, "Maturity includes the recognition that no one is going to see anything in us that we don't see in ourselves.... Joy is what happens when we allow ourselves to recognize how good things really are."

And when we can live from this joyful place, we unconsciously give others permission to do the same. Imagine a world where all curses were transformed into blessings, where we looked with inner and outer eyes that only saw order, righteousness and good – and not for a brief inspired moment – but as the natural state of continuous connection to our Source. Let's start now.

Internalize & Actualize:

1. Using the steps above, every day this week write down every negative thought you had about yourself. At the end of the week, look in the mirror and read them aloud. Pay attention to the language you use and the way you speak about yourself. If you wouldn't say these statements to someone else, then stop saying them to yourself.

   _____

   _____

   _____

2. Look through the statements you wrote down from the week. Take one that kept repeating or that was the harshest. Now counteract it with three to five positive statements. Write them below. Ideally do this for *every* negative statement you made during the week.

   _____

   _____

   _____

3. This one may be hardest as this may not *yet* be your reality. But the more you start to envision it, the sooner that shift will change. Write down how you want to see yourself and to do so, envision that you are speaking to yourself as a soul and not who you are in your body. If you could speak to your essence before you even came into this world, in your perfected state, what would you see and say?

    _____

    _____

    _____

PRACTICING UNILATERAL VIRTUE IN THE FACE OF EVIL

(*Pinchat*/Numbers 25:10 – 30:1)

"If you don't stand for something you will fall for anything."

- Gordon A. Eadie

Blaming the Jews

My husband was shaking his head as he was scrolling down the text on his cell phone. "Who do you think Greece blames for the collapse of its economy?" "I dunno…" I replied offhandedly, "Must be the Jews." I figured I was being sarcastic. My husband then read out loud the vilest invectives spewed by political and "religious" Greek leaders, laying the blame not just for Greece's financial woes, but nearly all of the problems of the world since time immemorial at our Jewish feet. "Who do you think is getting the blame for the shooting of police officers in Dallas?" I shot back, playing this sick game of "who do you think…" Israel, of course. It's always Israel. In twisted minds, dots connect in bizarre and irrational ways.

These days, the news, in general, seems pretty bad; the news related to Jews, however, is once again reaching unimaginable lows. Sadly, however, is it really anything new? The previous Torah portion, "*Balak*," is named after one of the most paranoid and mentally disordered anti-Semites recorded in the Torah. This week's Torah portion, "*Pinchat*," is named after the Jewish hero who foiled Balak's attempt to annihilate the Jews while they were still in in the dessert. Pinchat was not originally included in the priestly class, but as a result of his zealous courage, he was elevated into the priesthood and bestowed with an eternal covenant of peace, kinda like the Nobel Peace prize, but much better.

Is it a "coincidence," that *Pinchat* directly follows the Torah portion, *Balak*? I never noticed this before, and now I am wondering whether these two Torah portions are best understood as a pair, that somehow "evil" and "peace" are package deals. Like growth through adversity, Balak's plot to destroy the Jewish people gave Pinchat the opportunity to rise to the occasion, and in so doing, Pinchat changed the fate of the Jewish people as well as his own destiny.

Practicing Unilateral Virtue

When the news brings us daily reports of implacable hatred and inhuman brutality, how do we react with a response that is nevertheless rooted in humanity? How can we retain our humanity in the face of an evil that wants to seduce us away from it? And can we use that very evil to bring out our personal best?

Says Rick Hanson, a neuropsychologist famous for using neuroplasticity to create positivity in people's lives, "One of the hardest things to do is to remain reasonable, responsible, and ethical ourselves when others don't." In a challenging situation, how do you want to be? Can you live by your personal code even when it's hard? What is your code? What is your integrity system? What kind of honorable person are you moved to be from the inside out?

Personal Power

When we blame someone or something else for our perceived problems, then we are out-sourcing the solution as well. For example, if it were Balak's fault that the Jews in the desert were suffering, then only Balak could change the situation. This belief creates disempowerment, which is the root of the victim mentality. Pinchat, on the other hand, didn't waste any time on the "blame game." Instead, he took action where he could and focused on remedying the negative behavior he was witnessing in the Jewish people.

What is perhaps even more amazing is that he went against his nature to do what he did. It would be easy to think, "Well, I am no Pinchat. I'm not bold like that, daring and courageous." But neither was he! The text explains that he took after his grandfather, Aaron, whose temperament was compassionate and peace loving. And yet Pinchat killed, acting in complete opposition to his nature. And in so doing, he did what needed to be done. As explained by the Lubavitcher Rebbe, "He transcended his inborn instincts to bring peace between God and Israel."

Pinchat fought an external enemy by correcting an internal fault in the Jewish people. The very purpose of negativity is for us to change it. We change "it," however, when we change ourselves, like the slogan, "Think globally – act locally." When you work on yourself, you are affecting the world. If you stop feeding negativity anywhere, it will starve everywhere.

For example, when Jacob was preparing for his famous encounter with his brother, Esau, whom Jacob feared could still want to kill him, Jacob prepared in three ways: he brought gifts, he prayed, and he equipped himself for war. And so, dealing with evil is never a "one solution fits all" kind of approach. While politics and military operations may be necessary, at the same time, we must *also* regard the spiritual realm as every bit as real and powerful – if not more so.

Realistically, isn't that the realm that most of us can access anyway? The daily dose of bad news can depress you, enervate you, and leave you trembling with fear waiting for horror to strike. That is, however, precisely when we need to bring our A-Game.

May we use these times surrounded by the evil of modern-day Balaks to rise to the occasion and actualize our potential of unilateral virtue, integrity, and courage. We can all be winners of the peace prize, and thereby, we may change not only our own fate but also the destiny of the whole world.

Internalize & Actualize:

1. Think about a situation in your life where you began with a *"Balak"* situation and ended with a *"Pinchat"* one (something that started out negative and ended in a positive way). Looking back, do you think you appreciated the outcome even more because of the hard start?

_____

_____

_____

2. When have you gone against your nature and done what was needed in the moment, where the delay in thinking about it would have prevented you from doing it? What did you learn from the situation? Have you tapped into this part of yourself more often because you now know it is within you?

_____

_____

_____

3. We all deal with situations that we are convinced are the fault of another. What is something that you blame someone (or something) else for? What will change if you can assume responsibility? Even if you can't control what is happening or has happened, you can control how you respond and react to it. Write down three things you can do differently in this particular situation.

_____

_____

_____

THE DUAL NATURE OF
OUR STRENGTH

(*Mattot*/Numbers 30:2 – 32:42)

"We need a psychology of rising to the occasion."

- Martin Seligman

Staffs and Reeds

"Character cannot be developed in ease and quiet. Only through experience of trial and suffering can the soul be strengthened, vision cleared, ambition inspired, and success achieved." If anyone knew the truth of this, it would be the author of this quote - Helen Keller.

In the Torah portion, *"Mattot,"* the Jewish people were on the cusp of entering the Land of Israel. While this would be the joyful fulfillment of God's ancestral promise, it was not going to be all ease and quiet and "milk and honey." It was quite the opposite; actually, as the Jews who entered into the Land were headed into cycles of trial and suffering that would last for years to come.

At this critical time, God referred to the Jewish people as *"mattot"* which has the dual meaning of both "tribes" as well as "staffs." Wooden staffs are unbending, unyielding, straight and strong. Thus, God was imbuing the Jewish people with the very qualities they would need in light of the turmoil and challenges ahead.

While the word *mattot* is occasionally used, the most common word the Torah uses to refer to the Jewish tribes is not *mattot*, but *"shevatim."* Like the word *mattot, shevatim* also has a double definition – "tribes" or "reeds." Unlike wooden staffs, however, reeds are thin and flexible. Reeds are rooted, yet able to withstand external elements by being supple. In general, since God typically uses the word *shevatim,* one could surmise that embodying the qualities of the flexible reed is our natural or preferred state.

By referring to the Jewish tribes as *"mattot"* at this particular juncture, however, we should understand that sometimes - as in times of war, upheaval and chaos - we have to stiffen our resolve and embody a very different nature. There are times when being a reed does not serve us. There are times when being a reed hurts us. And in such times, we must become like *"mattot."* We must become a strong and solid staff. So, the question is: When do we become what?

Three Hours and Twelve Minutes

The news routinely brings horrors from abroad as well as close to home. As we were reeling with the news of the massacre in a gay bar in Florida that took place over a horrific three-hour period, we learned soon after of the brutal murder of a French police officer and his wife (in front of their three-year-old child). For twelve infinitely long minutes, the murderer chillingly filmed their torture, while issuing warnings to Europeans of Isis' intention to turn Europe into an imminent graveyard.

Not to be an alarmist, but in a split second, we can find ourselves face to face with momentous challenges. The flip side of adversity, however, is that it is the birthplace of greatness, for when we rise to the occasion of formidable challenges, we can achieve great heights. When confronting evil and hatred, we must stand as one with the strength of the wooden staff. As Winston Churchill said, "Never give in…never, never, never, in nothing great or small, large or petty, never give in except to convictions of honor and good sense. Never yield to force. Never yield to the apparently overwhelming might of the enemy."

Looking for the Good

On the other hand, when it comes to our interpersonal relationships and interactions with people outside of our comfort zone, we would be well served to be flexible, to put aside our differences and embrace our commonality. Eventually "close to home" as opposed to "over there" will be indistinct, as hatred anywhere must be perceived as hatred everywhere, and everyone's backyard becomes a global reality. When we empathetically feel the sufferings of others as our own, we will be inclined to commit acts of benevolence, compassion and bravery. And while we must keep our eyes open to the horrors of this world, it is just as important, if not more so, to see what is so very good. Otherwise, we will lose the best of what drives us forward.

In an article called, "The Optimism of Uncertainty," Howard Zinn wondered how it's possible to stay involved and happy in a world where the efforts of caring people often pale in comparison to what is done by those who have power. And he answers it thus:

> To be hopeful in bad times is not just foolishly romantic. It is based on the fact that human history is a history not only of cruelty, but also of compassion, sacrifice, courage, and kindness. What we choose to emphasize in this complex history will determine our lives. If we see only the worst, it destroys our capacity to do something. If we remember those times and places - and there are so many - where people have behaved magnificently, this gives us the energy to act, and at least the possibility of sending this spinning top of the world in a different direction. And if we do act, in however small way, we don't have to wait for some grand utopian future. The future is an infinite succession of presents, and to live now as we think human beings should live, in defiance of all that is bad around us, is itself a marvelous victory.[62]

Driving home, I was listening to the news. Overwhelmed with sadness and anxiety, I silently asked God to show me a sign of kindness and compassion. I thought of Fred Rogers' poignant reminiscence: "When I was a boy, and I would see scary things in the news, my mother would say to me, 'Look for the helpers. You will always find people who are helping.'" As if on cue, I noticed a homeless woman begging in the middle of a hot street, and I saw an arm shoot out of a car window to give her a bottle of water.

When we see pain and suffering, we must, even to the point of bending over backward, do what we can to ease it. When people hurt, we must heal. When it comes to the root causes of pain and suffering, however, and those who inflict it, we must stand tall against the inflictors. We must help. God tells us we have a dual nature. We must use our heads and hearts to know when to be what.

Internalize & Actualize:

1. Write down a challenging situation you are currently facing and think if you have been handling it like a staff or like a reed. Would it perhaps be better served by switching approaches? What do you feel will make the biggest impact in transforming this situation to the positive?

_____

_____

_____

2. When terrible things happen it is easy to lose sight of anything positive that is happening around us. Think about something difficult you have experienced, and then write down five good things that happened during this experience. They may pale in comparison, but focus on them. Then write down how you are feeling when you think about something uplifting alongside something so negative.

_____

_____

_____

3. Finding the good in those we struggle with is likewise a challenge. Think about someone you have a difficult time getting along with, and write down the characteristics and qualities that bother you about that person. Then alongside each aspect you find negative, write something that is positive about that quality (i.e., stubborn = someone who stands by his or her beliefs and feelings).

_____

_____

_____

THE JOURNEY OF THE JOURNEY
(*Matei*/Numbers 33:1 – 36:13)

"Every day is a journey, and the journey itself is home."

- Matsuo Basho

The Journey vs. the Destination

It was late at night when the phone rang. Not good. The caller ID was from my son. Definitely not good. As my son was leaving work after a night event, he noticed an open window in his building, and in closing it, the entire window fell out of the frame, hitting him on the head and rendering him temporarily unconscious. He was calling from a hospital located about an hour from me. I made it there in twenty-five minutes. Sometimes, a journey is only about reaching the destination. Other times, it's about what happens along the way.

The name of this week's Torah portion, *"Matei,"* means "journeys," and the Torah portion describes the forty-two stops (each of which is considered to be a journey unto itself) that the Jewish people experienced during the forty-year period between their leaving Egypt and entering the Land of Israel. As explained by the Baal Shem Tov, the founder of the Chassidic movement, "The forty-two 'stations' from Egypt to the Promised Land are replayed in the life of every individual Jew, as his soul journeys from its descent to earth at birth to its return to its Source." And in describing these journeys, the Torah uses two different phrases, but in the exact opposite word order: "their goings forth according to their journeys," and "their journeys according to their goings forth."

Rabbi Samson Raphael Hirsch explains that the first phrase, "their goings forth according to their journeys," is about the future destination. The very point of "going forth" is to experience the end game of the journey, in this case, to enter the Land of Israel, by leaving Egypt behind. This viewpoint is the big macro picture, as seen from God's perspective, and whether we understand it or not, each stop was a necessary part of an ultimate Divine plan.

The second phrase, "their journeys according to their goings forth," however, is the opposite end of the stick, where the point of the destination is primarily to create the experience of the journey, in this case, shedding and transcending the slave mentality of Egypt. This phrase is about our micro perspective of each stop, and how we see our journey, as we experience each new adventure in the "now" of our lives.

This is a lesson to us about our adventures in life. Each pause, every interruption or time we lose momentum and stay put in a particular place, is not taking us away from our journey, but rather is a journey in and of itself. For it is what we learn during these stops, or even setbacks, that propel us to move forward and help define or redefine the direction where we are going and ultimately where our journey will take us.

Finding the Balance

Optimal happiness is derived from combining these perspectives, by focusing goals towards an ultimate destination or result, while at the same time, smelling the proverbial roses of life along the way. And so it is spiritually as well. The number forty-two (from the forty-two stops) alludes to the mystical "Forty-two Letter Name of God." In mystical Judaism, this ineffable name refers to God's act of creation, as well as the unfolding of time. They are integral to each and have a mirror purpose.

Similarly, we experience and process the journeys of our lives from our limited human perspective. But at the same time, we also acknowledge that there is also a Divine Hand guiding us along, that there is a bigger picture and that the events in our lives and across the span of our lives (and lifetimes) are connected. Sometimes, we catch a glimpse of it; other times it's completely hidden from view.

To live with purpose, we need to have a goal in mind, where each step heads in that direction. Yet we never want to forget that there are lessons to learn along the way and that each step can help guide and determine how we reach our goal (or maybe even redefine it). Journeys are not merely physical sojourns but are also meant to be inward spiritual experiences.

Internalize & Actualize:

1. Write down a goal you want to reach. Why is that goal important to you? How do you think accomplishing it will change your life or make you better as a person?

   _____

   _____

   _____

2. What are some of the challenges or setbacks you have had in trying to reach this goal? Write them down and then write down how you can view these as journeys within the journey to your ultimate goal.

   _____

   _____

   _____

3. Now think about a goal you have accomplished. When reflecting specifically on the process of getting there, what lessons did you learn from the process itself and what skills did you use throughout it to stay focused and motivated while dealing with setbacks and stops? How can you apply those skills to the current goal you are trying to reach?

   _____

   _____

   _____

-DEVARIM-
DEUTERONOMY

THE EASY LIFE VERSUS THE MEANINGFUL LIFE

*(Devarim/*Deuteronomy 1:1 – 3:22)*

"Do not pray for an easy life. Pray for the strength to endure a difficult one."

- Bruce Lee

In one of the most famous mass performance reviews in written history, the book of *Devarim* (Deuteronomy) starts out with Moses doing a recap and overview of the Jewish people since they left Egypt; and the review was hardly favorable. In the re-telling of one of the lowest moments of that period, the "incident of the spies," (where the Jewish people were afraid of entering the Land of Israel after hearing the fearful report from the infamous spies), Moses pointedly reminded the people how they spoke slander against God when they said: "Because of God's hatred for us did he take us out of the land of Egypt, to deliver us into the hand of the Amorite to destroy us."[63]

This is tantamount to claiming that the whole thing was a setup from the start, that God freed us from Egypt, only to deliver us into the hands of a much worse enemy and certain death. We, of course, have the comfortable vantage point of having read "The Book" (and we saw The Movie too), so we know the story ends with the Jewish people about to enter the Land of Israel. But, in defense of the masses, manipulated into a state of terror by the spies, can we empathize with their pain when they "claimed" God hated them? What was really going on?

The Longing Underneath the Complaint

When our children come home from school, smarting from a bad grade or being disciplined, and they cry out with unwavering certainty, "My teacher hates me!" are they making a statement of objective fact or are they expressing an unspoken fear of not being loved by the teacher? What is the unexpressed longing underneath their complaints? One Sunday, my husband and I had independent plans for the afternoon. When I came home, he was agitated and demanded to know what had taken me so long. I had no idea that his plans had fallen through and so I reacted to what I thought was an unfair and irrational criticism with ballistic verbal weapons of my own, and we spent the rest of the evening disconnected and polarized. Later on, I was able to soften when I realized that underneath the blame and criticism was a longing for connection and a fear of vulnerability, and we were able to have a conversation that re-connected us.

While it's very challenging to remain centered, conscious and non-reactive when someone is bitterly complaining, look under the hood of a complaint – *especially* an irrational one - and you will likely find someone who is insecure, wondering if he or she is loved. (Just to be clear, I don't regard terrorism and anti-Semitism as "bad behavior masquerading as a cry for love." Evil is not masquerading as a call to love.) On the other hand, disciplining myself to ignore *how* a message is conveyed so as not to lose sight of the underlying expression of a legitimate need, is a choice I try to make in my relationships.

If God Only Loved Us...

Therefore, when seen in that favorable and compassionate light, you could consider the irrational complaints and accusations the Jewish people made against God, as evidence of very insecure people questioning their relationship with God. In *their* minds, in *their* logic, it made sense that if God loved them, he could have kicked the Egyptians out of Egypt and let the Jews live free and safe in the fertile Nile delta. If God valued the Jewish people, why were *they* the ones wandering in the desert? Why were *they* attacked and beset by those trying to destroy them? And why did *they* have to face years of battle to establish their homeland? At Mt. Sinai, God called us "His Beloved." Really? Is this what love looks like?

When my husband was a little boy, he lived in the DP (Displaced Person's) Camps in Germany after the war. "The bad Germans lost the war," he was told. And yet it was these "bad" Germans who walked around freely, seemingly doing as they pleased, while he could only peer in bewilderment at them from behind barbed wire, confined to the grounds of a concentration camp that was hastily upgraded to house the Jews that had nowhere else to go. The little boy was confused. Is this what winning looks like?

And when we read the news today, with worldwide terror a commonplace event, and anti-Semitism rising up with a terrifying velocity, isn't it possible to wonder whether God really loves us as well? Like – what's the deal? So, are life's challenges proof of God's hate or evidence of His love?

A Mother's Blessing

I heard a lecture by Rebbetzin Tzipporah Heller, who asked us to consider why we bless our daughters every Friday night, to be like Sarah, Rebecca, Rachel, and Leah? After all, how were our foremothers so "blessed"? They had lives of unbelievable challenges, hardships, and adversities, (such as multiple kidnappings and infertility), that seemed much more like curses than blessings, as well as having to endure dysfunctional family dynamics that would compete with any sensational tabloids we see today. So why would I want any of that for my daughter? Wouldn't it make more sense for me to find a better role model, a female figure of merit, yet one who had it somewhat easy?

And so consider this choice - a beloved and famous young woman who has not just the perfect easy life, but the perfect body, long flowing hair, flawless skin, loyal friends, adoring faithful boyfriend, great clothes, cute pink car – all complete with its own carrying case. In case you didn't figure it out, it's Barbie. Suddenly, the catchy pop lyrics sound in my head: *"I'm a Barbie girl. In a Barbie world. Life in plastic. It's fantastic."* Now, how does that sound as a utopia? And yet, that is what the Jews were complaining about. In essence, if God loved them, then they should have been able to live like Barbie and Ken – but in Egypt.

Life's Bigger Purpose

God had – and has – other plans for us. He wants us to have a real, meaningful and fulfilling life. God wants our lives to shimmer with transcendence and holiness, endowed with purpose and service. God wants us to have a life where we overcome adversity, where we choose and grow. As Rilke said, "The purpose of life is to be defeated by greater and greater things."

You can't move up the ladder by being a plastic doll or yearning for a life of ease. And so, while our forefathers and mothers didn't have comfortable lives, they had profoundly meaningful and spiritual lives, lives that charted our very course and destiny, and whose qualities are embedded in our spiritual DNA. When we don't confuse the good life with an easy life, then we can embrace challenges as a means of self-discovery. And when we don't expect our lives to be simple, then we can tap into our significance. In giving us the Torah, you could say that God was the first life coach ever – exhorting us to live our lives by design and not by default. That sure looks like love to me!

And therefore, while the complaint of the Jews in the desert against God was perhaps understandable, in the end, it was ultimately unjustifiable - because the longing underneath the complaint equated easy street with God's love, and adversity and challenge with God's "hatred." So even if its origin was fear, such thinking was distorted and immature. And when others were looped into the negativity, these complaints were rightfully deserving of Moses' derision.

Whenever you may face individual and national challenges, do not fall prey to insecurity that doubts God's love and connection and think that life is a "set-up." Instead, ponder the ineffable survival and spirit of the Jewish people over the millennia, and remind yourself of the times in your life where you have endured suffering that led to blessings or growth.

Internalize & Actualize:

1. Think of a time that you acted out or behaved in a certain manner, which really was a defense mechanism for how you were truly feeling. Write down the adjectives to describe your behavior, and then alongside it, write down the adjectives that represented what was really going on in your head and heart.

   _____

   _____

   _____

2. With the above in mind, think about a situation where someone else behaved towards you or responded with negative behavior that was similar to yours. Knowing that your behavior did not represent how you were actually feeling, rewrite that situation and how you feel towards that person when you believe that their true feelings came from hurt, fear, insecurity (etc.), rather than rudeness, anger or blame (etc.).

   _____

   _____

   _____

3. When in your life did someone push you well out of your comfort zone, and as much as you may have resented it at the time, you eventually came to recognize strengths in yourself you would not have discovered without that challenge? How can you apply this lesson to situations you are now facing where you would rather take the "easy" path than the one less traveled?

   _____

   _____

   _____

WHO'S GONNA KNOW?

*(Va'etchanan/*Deuteronomy 3:23 – 7:11)*

*"Alignment begins with a constituency of one.... Our level
of effectiveness, contribution and integrity of work and life
are in direct correlation with our level of integration, self-
actualization and total alignment of body, mind and spirit."*

- Kristin S. Kaufman

Legend has it that a rabbi, who had purchased a camel from an
Arab, subsequently found a large precious jewel in the camel's saddlebag.
Purportedly over the objections of his friends, the rabbi held fast to the
Torah law of returning lost objects and brought the jewel back to the Arab,
who effusively praised the rabbi for his integrity and honesty – *and upon
his God* – who so commands it.

Once upon a time, I was loading groceries into my car, and I realized
that a case of water that I had put on the lower rack of my shopping cart
hadn't been scanned and paid for. Accompanying me was a friend who had
needed a ride to the market, and she suggested that I just keep the water.
"Who's gonna know?" she reasoned.

Remembering the story of the rabbi and the lost jewel, however, I
returned to the supermarket, back to the same cashier who had checked
me out, and explained what had happened. And then I waited. For the
heaps of praise for me - and for my God - who instructs me to act with the

utmost integrity and honesty. Instead, the cashier wordlessly and without so much as changing the expression on her face, scanned the case of water and waited for me to slide my credit card. This wasn't exactly the reaction I was hoping for, but I had to laugh at myself. *Wow, Hanna, you were expecting a congressional medal of honor for not stealing?*

And if my behavior made no impression on the cashier, who, after all, had nothing to gain by it, was it noted, I wondered, in the Heavenly annals above? There's a scene in one of my favorite movies, *Family Man*, where a girl is buying items at a convenience store and hands the cashier a ten-dollar bill. The cashier says to her, "Out of twenty, here's your change." Realizing that the cashier had made a mistake and had given her back too much money, the girl hesitated. "Is something wrong?" the clerk asked, but the girl shook her head and walked out of the store. The cashier was none other than an angel, and after the girl had left, he shook his head and recorded the infraction in his "heavenly notebook," disappointed at how she had failed the test, selling out for a few measly dollars.

The Need for External Validation

While we hope that someone, somewhere takes notice whenever we "do the right thing," as long as we are driven by the need for that external recognition, we are vulnerable and can be inconsistent. For example, whenever possible, I try to make way for drivers who need to get in my lane or make turns, etc., sometimes incurring the anger of drivers behind me as I hold up traffic momentarily. But when that driver then fails to acknowledge my "kindness" by so much as a wave of the hand, I feel "used." Such disappointments can lead to thoughts as silly as, "I was nice for nothing," and shifting my behavior towards others people, like maybe the next time I won't be so kind. That is not a good thing.

The Case for Internal Validation

And so, returning a case of water to the supermarket shouldn't be about scoring brownie points in heaven - or even getting any acknowledgment here on earth. The deepest answer to the question, "*Who's gonna know?*"

is, *"Me."* I would have known that I had acted inappropriately. *I* would have understood that my behavior was out of synch with my God-given values. And *I* would have known that my behavior had just made the world a tiny bit darker.

In the Torah portion, *Va'etchanan,* Moses has only a few weeks left to teach and inspire the Jewish people, who were about to cross over to the Land of Israel, without him. Like a father imparting his last words of wisdom to a child who is about to journey away from home, so did Moses teach the Jewish people the deepest lesson of them all –*"Hear O' Israel, the Lord is thy God, the Lord is One."*

And so, should we strive to be. One. Inside and out. No matter what. And this applies to when we get what we want, and even, if not more so, when we don't. Keep in mind that Moses had aspired to enter the Land of Israel more than anything. But he accepted that it was not meant to be. And rather than being bitter or hurt, he focused on the need for unity amongst the Jewish people and the unity of the Jewish people with God.

Unlike living in the miraculous and protected cocoon of the desert, where God overtly provided everything for the Jewish people, they were going to be living so-called "normal everyday lives." They would be on the battlefield, in the marketplace and in the privacy of their homes. Unlike being under the watchful eye of Moses, or the scrutiny of God who meted out swift and strict justice in the desert, the Jewish people would find themselves in many situations where they could reasonably ask themselves, *"Who's gonna know?"* Moses wanted every individual to have the strength of inner conviction to be able to answer that question unwaveringly: *"God will – but so will I."*

Internalize & Actualize:

1. What is something you have done or do that you hope others don't know about? If you were to get caught in the "act" of thinking, saying or doing this thing, how would it make you feel?

2. Now, what is something you have done or do because it is inherently good, positive or helpful? How does it make you feel when you do this? Does it matter to you if others know you are doing this?

_____

_____

_____

3. Commit to doing positive actions that you do for another person with complete anonymity. You are doing this solely because it is positive and not for external recognition. What is it that you can begin doing immediately, how will it help the other, and record over the course of the week how it makes you feel. (It can be small like getting someone a coffee at work or making sure to say "good morning" to strangers.)

_____

_____

_____

46

THE SECRET WEAPON TO A CULTURE OF HATE

(*Eikev*/Deuteronomy 7:12 – 11:25)

"Hatred paralyzes life. Love releases it.
Hatred confuses life. Love harmonizes it.
Hatred darkens life. Love illuminates it."

- Martin Luther King, Jr.

Community "Standards"

The response I got from Facebook hit me like a punch in the stomach. I had joined about 26,000 other people in asking Facebook to take down the "I Hate Israel" page, as Facebook has a so-called "policy" that purports to disallow hate speech, or attacks on individuals or groups based on ethnicity, national origin, religion, etc. I thought the "I Hate Israel" easily fell squarely within those parameters. I thought Facebook took its policies seriously, and so I thought it was a no-brainer. Isn't an "I Hate…" page inherently hateful?

When I got the e-mail reply from Facebook that after review, the page "didn't violate its community's standards," I was disappointed. So, who is the face behind Facebook? Is it like the Wizard of Oz – *"The great and all powerful Facebook shall now answer your question."*

Seriously - who made that judgment call and generated that reply?

And just whose community are we talking about? Because any community whose sensibilities are not violated by an "I Hate Israel" page - is certainly not a community of mine.

The Need to Belong

Why do we want to belong to community anyway? Apparently, it is a fundamental, innate and hard-wired need that we have, this "need to belong," and to belong to something bigger than ourselves. According to Abraham Maslow, all humans have five needs, but they are hierarchical. After the basic, bottom needs of physiological survival and safety are satisfied, the next human need is "love and belonging."

Belonging feels safe and good emotionally. Practically, we couldn't survive without sharing the resources, strengths and skills and others. And psychologically, belonging to a community can give us a sense of identity, direction, perspective and moral strength. While there's nothing wrong with the need, it's how we go about satisfying it that matters. We have to be careful and conscious about what and to whom we attach ourselves.

Some communities inspire and promote individual growth and potential while providing the means to serve something greater than us. Other communities act as a mechanism to keep people mired in conformity and a mob mentality, furthering the cause of hatred. In such communities, like the so-called "Facebook community," it is not a "community violation" to publically stand for "hate." Other communities take it further and applaud and honor hatred as an ideal state of being.

Being Fully Human Is to Be Guided by Divinity

Hillel encapsulated the Torah with the famous phrase, "What is hateful to you, do not do to others; now go and learn." Sadly, for many people, inhumane, brutal and sick behavior is not hateful. It would be simplistic to believe that they just lack a moral compass. Or worse - that they are amoral sociopaths unable to know the difference between right and wrong. To the contrary – violence is a calculated means to serve their mission. And when supported and applauded by community, violence is more than a distorted virtue; it's a "moral" obligation.

Thus, it is not a foregone conclusion, and so Hillel is exhorting us to "go and learn" what in fact should be hateful to a properly-calibrated human being. We can't forget that there is a spiritual component to the need to belong. How do we meet that need, however? Says Hillel, "Go and learn Torah," - and in so doing, let Divinity guide you in living to the fullness of your humanity.

Desert Clarity

In the Torah portion, "*Eikev*," Moses, who is but a few weeks away from his death, is instructing and cautioning the Jewish people about the future challenges of facing life in the Land of Israel. In the desert, God was palpable. Daily, overt miracles satisfied all of our needs. And we saw strict judgment in action. Mess with God, and you were zapped. Mess with the Jewish people, and you went down. Evil was summarily dealt with. There was clarity.

Once we would leave that cocoon to live in the "real world," however, that clarity could fade, and then we would be vulnerable to internal confusion and beset by external enemies. And that is why Moses was stressing the importance over and over to love God, to attach ourselves to God, to emulate God and to walk in His ways. "Be kind to each other; take care of the needy, the orphan, the poor, the widow...." Because the more we learn and emulate what is holy and shun what is hateful, the closer we are to God. And the closer we are to God, the more palpable and manifest is His presence.

The idea is to create "desert clarity" now, in our everyday lives, and to create the channel to bring down the Divine protection that was given us in the wilderness. At the end of *Eikev*, Moses tells us flat out – "Heed my words, and your enemies will vanish. You will tread where you will, and no man will stand up to you." Really, could this advice be any timelier than today?

Internalize & Actualize:

1. What kind of community are you a part of? Do you feel at home in your community? Do you feel accepted and celebrated? If so, why? If not, what is missing that you would need to feel supported and included?

   _____

   _____

   _____

2. When in your life have you left a restrictive situation with a lot of rules, structure and consequences followed by a period of freedom, such as leaving home and going to college? Looking back, during which period were you healthier and more stable. Why?

   _____

   _____

   _____

3. If learning is what keeps us balanced and centered, what kind of learning do you do on a regular basis? Better yet, do you have a daily practice devoted to your growth? Learning could easily seem like an "extra" and something we are too busy for, yet it is essential. Write down how you can start incorporating some learning, even just ten minutes a day, into your daily life. What do you want to focus on? How are you going to do this learning and what do you hope you will get out of it?

   _____

   _____

   _____

BELIEVING IS SEEING

(*Re'eh*/Deuteronomy 11:26 – 16:17)

"What we do see depends mainly on what we look for.
In the same field the farmer will notice the crop,
the geologists the fossils, botanists the flowers,
artists the coloring, sportsmen the cover for the game.
Though we may all look at the same things,
it does not all follow that we should see them."

- John Lubbock

There's a saying – "You can talk about politics and religion. Or you can have friends." How many gatherings end on a sour note, and how many conversations end with hurt feelings when conversations turn to these subjects? It's frightening how quickly a discussion can go from civil to caustic, each side usually advocating a one-dimensional version of reality as the uncontroverted truth.

Perception has come to be synonymous with reality, but perception depends less on what we see and more on who we are. Says Robertson Davies, "The eye sees only what the mind is prepared to comprehend." What we see when we look, therefore, is a choice.

Perception Bias

A few years ago, the theory of "Perception Bias" was tested by placing Joshua Bell, a world-class violinist, in the DC Metro.[64] Playing some of the most sublime music ever composed, on a violin worth several million dollars, Joshua Bell played in front of thousands of streaming commuters, who wouldn't even look his way. Curious toddlers, not yet permeated with perception bias, and who wanted to stop and listen, were yanked along by impatient parents, not interested in a "subway musician" whose tickets for his performance that evening sold for over a hundred dollars a pop.

While our brains take in billions of bits of information per second, our brains select an infinitesimal sliver – out of all the possible realities to consider - and then, our bias further tells us how to interpret that sliver. It's all a choice – believe it or not. Thus, our perceptions are biased. But that's not necessarily a bad thing.

This week's Torah portion, *"Re'eh,"* which means "see," begins thus: "See, I present before you today a blessing and a curse."[65] *Re'eh* goes on to explain what we shall and shall not do as we enter the Land of Israel, and it is a recap of many of the laws already given. Like "the talk" many parents give children before sending them to college, reminding the child that independence, freedom and a new environment do not permit the abandonment of the values and teachings the child received at home, so does God remind us that we are a holy nation about to enter a holy land. And we must conduct ourselves accordingly.

God knows that perception bias inevitably shapes our perceptions. Therefore, God tells us: "Safeguard and hearken to all these words which I command you, in order that it may be well with you and your children after you forever, when you do what is good and right in the eyes of the Lord, your God."[66] Therefore, God exhorts us to look at reality not with our eyes, but with Godly eyes. For when we see reality with that kind of spiritual clarity, then our choices will follow naturally and logically as an expression of that vision. So how can we put this to use in our day to day lives?

Making Perception Bias Work for You

First, we must decide what it is we want to see; because we always and inevitably find what we are looking for. If no one is without perception bias, then we have to make it work *for* us instead of *against* us, because it's about the choices we make.

Do you want to find something to criticize in a person? You will. Do you want to find the negative in a situation? You will. Thoreau said that a faultfinder will find fault - even in paradise. On the other hand, do you want to see the good in a person or a situation? You will. Do you wish you could see your life as filled with blessings? You can. "Whether you think you can or you can't, you're right."[67] The question you have to answer for yourself is what kind of life do you want to have?

The Torah is called the Tree of Life, and a tree has many branches and many leaves. Look at it with new eyes, with Godly eyes. Look at it with the deliberate intention of seeing something good, of seeing something in a new light, anything really, that will help you be a better, kinder person, that will help you get a little bit closer to God and a little more loving of your fellow man. Just one leaf. And then choose it and act consistently with your choice. When you learn the meaning of choosing the blessings life has to offer, seeing the good becomes a no-brainer.

Internalize & Actualize:

1. Write down five things you don't like about yourself. Be honest and blunt. Now, right next to those rewrite those very five things into something positive. This is not about finding five different things you do like, but about liking the five things you don't like (i.e., "I am fat and hate my body" versus, "my body has carried and birthed my children and given them life").

———————————————————

———————————————————

———————————————————

2. Since we see what we are looking for, what are some of things you want to be seeing in your life? Are you looking in the right places for them? Are you looking with the right eyes to find them? Why or why not? How can you see differently?

   _____

   _____

   _____

3. Do others see you the way you want to be seen? What can you do differently so that when people look at you they see your beauty and the amazing person you truly are?

   _____

   _____

   _____

JUSTICE, JUSTICE SHALL
YOU PURSUE

(*Shoftim*/Deuteronomy 16:18 – 21:9)

*"I am the Lord, who exercises kindness, justice and
righteousness on earth, for in these I delight."*

- Jeremiah 9:24

Necessary Repetition

If you are a Jewish kid who graduated from law school – and actually
got a job - chances are that your proud parents gave you a picture to
hang on the wall of your office (or windowless cubicle) with the famous
quote, "Justice, Justice, Shall You Pursue." These words come right at the
beginning of the Torah portion, "*Shoftim*," meaning, "Judges."

As I type the words of this chapter, programmed to assume that I
have made a typo by repeating the same word, Microsoft Word highlights
the second "justice" in red for me – alerting me to my "mistake." If only
Moses had a laptop with spell check and typo correction, he could have
fixed a lot of "typos," because we see this same duplication in other places
in the Torah; such as when God calls out "Abraham-Abraham," or "Jacob-
Jacob," or "Moses-Moses." Is it bad editing, or rather, is it significant and
transformational? And is there a connection between the phrase "justice-
justice" and the duplicative names?

When God calls out: "Abraham-Abraham" or "Moses-Moses," etc., the sentiment is tender and intimate. Think of cuddling a baby or speaking the name of your beloved – we often say their names twice, because, well, once is just not enough to convey the depth of the emotions we feel at that moment. Repeating the first name in that manner is a verbal caress.

As Above – So Below

There is another concept at work in this double name-calling that is more applicable here, and that is the idea of "as above, so is below." There is a heavenly version of ourselves, and there is an earthly version of ourselves. The heavenly version represents our potential, the person we could be. The earthly version, on the other hand, is who we are and how we are showing up in the world. Think of two portraits: one is hanging on heaven's walls, and the other one is you, walking around, as the expression of the sum of your choices.

When God calls out their double names, we are to understand that in the case of Abraham, Jacob and Moses, these two versions were aligned. There is not a "heavenly Abraham" in contrast to an "earthly Abraham." The Abraham above was the same as below – congruent and unified between his ideas and his actions.

Permission to Be Human

However, that's not true for most of us. We're here to work and narrow the gap and come as close to that heavenly portrait of ourselves and our potential as possible. Living up to our potential, being congruent and authentic, and behaving externally in a way that mirrors our highest internal values, is admittedly a big challenge. But as a rabbi used to say to me, "we are all works in progress."

Permission Denied

But that idea doesn't work well with *ideals*. A society where earthly justice is really out of sync with heavenly justice is not a "society in progress;" rather, it is an *unjust* society. What we can tolerate in ourselves and on an individual level is intolerable when perpetrated on a grand societal scale. For justice to be "just," it has to be authentic, congruent and actualized. Just like you can't be a little bit pregnant, you can't have just a little bit of justice.

Righteous Justice

But who must act justly? We must act justly. And who enacts justice? We must enact it. It's in our hands. So, can imperfect beings ever create human justice that aligns with heaven? We imagine Divine justice as strict and severe and we tremble at the idea of facing the Heavenly Court because that is one tough bench to get over.

Maybe there is another alignment going on. In Hebrew, the word, "*tzedek*," which means "justice," also means "righteousness." Perhaps the dual use of the word "justice" means that we cannot pursue "justice" without also being "righteous." That would be perverted justice. Think of the Nuremberg Laws that legitimized the Nazi regime. They were "codes of law," but utterly lacking righteousness, and in no way aligned with heaven. And we cannot think we are "righteous" unless we are also "just." Yann Martel, the author of *Life of Pi*, has said:

> These people walk by a widow deformed by leprosy, walk by children dressed in rags living in the street, and they think, 'Business as usual.' But if they perceive a slight against God, it is a different story. Their faces go red, their chests heave mightily, they sputter angry words. The degree of their indignation is astonishing. Their resolve is frightening.

This hypocrisy is perverted righteousness. The Hebrew word "*tzedaka*," which means "charity," comes from the same word, "*tzedek*," (justice/righteousness). Thus, unless righteousness is rooted in kindness, in compassion, being a giver and caring for the poor and needy, etc., it is not "just." For being "right with God" - but not with your fellow man - is not aligned with heaven.

In the Torah portion of *Shoftim*, "justice" is not a single word, because it is not a single concept. The double word is its own congruency. That's the alignment to strive for – justice that is righteous and righteousness that is just. As Robert Frost wisely observed, "Nothing can make injustice just but mercy."

And when we pursue that kind of justice here on earth, we are not only closing the gap between our earthly and heavenly selves, but maybe we are, in fact, mirroring the Heavenly court. If only we could create such a society and live in such a world, truly, wouldn't it be like heaven on earth? Now, how transformational is that?

Internalize & Actualize:

1. Can you think of a time you were "just," but not "righteous"? Meaning, you may have done the "right" thing but at the "wrong" cost? What was the outcome? In hindsight, how would you have handled it differently?

   _____

   _____

   _____

2. What about a time you may have been "righteous," but not "just"? You may have had the right intentions, but still did the "wrong" thing. How could you have handled that differently?

   _____

   _____

   _____

3. How would you describe the "you" that is earthly, that is below? Now how would you describe the "you" that is heavenly, above? What are some very practical ways that you can bridge the gap between the two of them?

   _____

   _____

   _____

THE POWER OF NO

(*Ki Teitzei*/Deuteronomy 21:10 – 25:19)

"Until you learn how to confidently say No to so many things, you shall always say Yes to so many things. The real summary of a regretful life is a life that failed to balance Yes and No."

- Ernest Agyemang Yeboah

I like to have guests at my Shabbat table, and depending on the themes of the weekly Torah portions, the table discussions can get a little heated. If you are apt to read the Torah and be offended, then welcome to the Torah portion, "*Ki Teitzei.*" *Ki Teitzei* means, "when you go out to war with your enemies," and it opens with the rules a man must obey when coming across a "beautiful woman on the battlefield." Since the Jewish people were getting ready to leave the desert and enter the Promised Land where they would be engaging in battles for years to come, this was a very likely scenario.

So, what were the rules? Could he rape her? *No.* Could he keep or sell her as a slave? *No.* Could he cut her head off and tweet the video? *Definitely not.* What, then, *could* a man in those circumstances do?

He could simply leave her where she was, or if he desired her, he had to bring her home, and wait during a cooling-off period where the enticement of her looks would diminish by stripping the woman of her finery, her ornaments and her ability to look seductive. During that time, the man could not touch her, but afterward, if he is still desired her, he had to marry her – or else he was required to set her free and compensate her for her "ordeal."

"But what if the woman didn't want to marry the guy?" you could ask. "Didn't she have a say in the matter? And she had no choice about being confined in his home for 30 days in a degrading way while he made up his mind about marrying her?" From these facts, one could reasonably conclude that this is sexist and horrible, since any system which could force a woman to marry against her will, is unquestionably offensive.

One response is to put this in the context of the ancient world. According to commentators, in anticipation of battle, women would put on finery and make themselves beautiful to entice Jewish men, because winding up with a "nice Jewish guy" was a heckuva lot better than their other choices. Also, compared to the battle ethic of the ancient world (your typical rape, murder, and pillage) the Torah scenario is positively enlightened and compassionate. Thanks to ISIS, and their ilk, I no longer have to contextualize this. Has anyone noticed that the "ancient world" is not so "ancient" anymore?

The Power of Emotional Mastery

But there is a much more profound response to these objections. The major theme of *Ki Teitzei* has to do with emotional mastery, to having thoughtful and reasoned responses to emotionally charged situations. And so, a deeper read of "when you go out to war with your enemies" could be this: "when you go out to war.... with *yourself*," referring to the struggle with your internal aspects that are base, unbridled and unbounded.

The purpose of the laws of "the beautiful captive" is not to result in an orderly marriage; rather, they are to prevent the marriage in the first place. The very objective of the process is to give the guy time to see the woman – not as a mere beautiful object – but as her authentic self. He has to be able to picture her as the mother of his children and someone who will be by his side for the rest of his life. He has to see her as compatible with his Jewish values and lifestyle.

He has to see her as not just satisfying his desire for instant gratification in the immediate present but as a total commitment to the future. And if she is not to be a full-fledged wife, then she can't be something other, like a slave. Rather, she must be compensated and set free.

213

The Power of Choice

In the last few weeks of his life, Moses was cramming in his final words of advice, and so the laws of *Ki Teitzei* come one after another. To what end? As slaves in Egypt, the Jewish people were not free to say "no" to the Pharaoh, and thus they had little to no free will. In the desert, the Jewish people lived with "strict justice," meaning that punishment was quickly and visibly meted out. While they had free will, they also had the clarity of cause and effect, and so if you said "no" to God's laws, you weren't going to be around long to brag about it.

Once the Jewish people would leave the desert, however, and live in the Promised Land, it was going to be an entirely different story - and that was Moses' concern. They would not be slaves to anyone; nor would they live with "desert clarity." They would have to figure out on their own how to say "no" to that which should be negated in their lives.

And that is where emotional mastery comes in. Torah doesn't permit us to have whatever we want, just because we want it. We cannot discard someone from our lives improperly or divest them of rights to suit our emotional needs. We can't put things together that don't belong together, and we can't make admixtures of things that deny the unique individuality, needs, and purpose of all living things. Each person and each situation are due carefully circumscribed borders of protection.

Understanding and respecting the sensitivities, the boundaries and the proper uses of all organisms – whether human, animal or even vegetable - is the basis of mastery over those emotional urges, which could cause us to violate someone or something else.

The Power of Yes

So, the battle is between you – and you – to develop healthy ways of dealing with exclusion. Certain things, certain people, and certain situations simply do not belong in our lives, nor do they belong with each other. It's about understanding the "Law of Exclusion" and going to war against that which blurs our boundaries.

A slave cannot say "no." Only a human being with autonomy and free will say "no." And that ability is precisely what makes a "yes" so powerful, so meaningful. Therefore, saying "no" to that which will bring you down is saying "yes" to that which can elevate you, make you grow, and sanctify your life. And that is certainly worth fighting for.

Internalize & Actualize:

1. In what ways are you at war with yourself? Are you winning or losing the battles?

_____

_____

_____

2. Is there a situation you are currently dealing with that you are reacting to in an emotionally inappropriate way? This week try to remove yourself from it, and then, with some distance, revisit how you are thinking and feeling and note if anything has changed.

_____

_____

_____

3. What is a part of your life that shouldn't be? How can you begin to separate yourself from it (or from that person) that is unhealthy or toxic for you? Recognizing that something or someone doesn't belong is the first step in the process.

_____

_____

_____

DON'T BE A BASKET CASE

(*Ki Tavo*/Deuteronomy 26:1 – 29:9)

"Build upon strengths and weaknesses will gradually take care of themselves."

- Joyce C. Lock

Step-by-Step Instructions

Words serve a purpose. Nothing in the Torah is superfluous or incredibly obvious. Therefore, when I notice the repeated use of a word that tells me something seemingly unnecessary, I take that as a challenge to find the deeper meaning.

The Torah portion, "*Ki Tavo*," starts by describing the laws of "*bikkurim*," which are the procedures for bringing the first fruits to the Priests in the Temple. But the description seems like it was written for children. We are commanded to place our fruits into a "basket," and then, when we get to the Temple, we are told that the priest will take our "basket" from our hand.

Really? Exactly how many container choices existed in the ancient world that would permit a person to transport fruit a long distance in the desert? And am I a child that I have to be micromanaged to "put my fruits in a basket and now hand the basket to the nice man in the Temple?" How is this meaningful, and what relevance can this possibly have to my life today?

Signature Strengths

While the Land of Israel produces many fruits and vegetables, only the seven species for which the Land of Israel is specifically praised for in the Torah, are brought to the Temple. Israel is "a land of wheat, barley, grapevines, figs, and pomegranates; a land of oil, olives and date honey."[68] You could say that mystically, these seven species are the Land of Israel's "Signature Strengths."

We all have certain positive traits, qualities, and abilities. There is a subset of these attributes, however, known as our "Signature Strengths" that comprise those unique combinations of abilities that when utilized, empower us to make our lives happier, more meaningful and fulfilled. These strengths are not about "should" and "could;" but rather, those positive aspects of ourselves that we are in our bones and where we can't be any other way even if we tried. As fundamental to our core as they are, however, sadly, we don't always know what these strengths are, and therefore, they are underutilized.

To uncover them, you don't have to spend years in therapy or travel to the Himalayas. You need only go on-line to the website from the University of Pennsylvania, "Authentic Happiness," click on the questionnaire tab and take the "VIA (Values in Action) Strengths Test."[69] Really – do it and you will get to know yourself in a different way.

Merely knowing your "Signature Strengths" however, is not enough. You have to be conscious and deliberate about it. When the farmer went into his fields and noticed the first buds to break, the first flower blossoms to emerge, and then the developing fruit, he tied a cord around the fruit and proclaimed that it was designated as a first fruit to be brought to the Temple. Otherwise, how could he know which fruits were which when he was harvesting? Therefore, we have to notice, pay attention, and honor our "Signature Strengths," so as to be able to draw on them.

As for a basket, which is lightweight, has holes for ventilation, and allows the fruit to lie in it without getting bruised, etc., we have to "carry" our strengths in a way that they are properly nurtured and used. All strengths have a flip-side that can become a weakness. For example, one of my strengths is creativity, and I get flooded with ideas. But many fall by the wayside as I get easily bored by the tedious minutia of implementation. Leadership is a strength – but it can also disempower others. Kindness is a strength, but it can also enable dysfunction and blind us to problems, etc. You get the idea.

Utilizing strengths to accomplish goals and develop resilience is efficacious and empowering. But we must be conscious and bounded, so as not to use our strengths in a way that hurts us – and others. When we hand the basket to the priest – who takes it from our hand - the idea is that we are using our strengths in the service of others, in connection with something bigger than ourselves, and as part of our relationship to God. Then it becomes an act of transcendence, which gives our lives deeper meaning, fulfillment, and purpose. It is the difference between being self-serving and serving God.

And that is the essence of "*bikkurim,*" to understand that everything we have is from God. Your "Signature Strengths" are a gift from God to you. But how you use your "Signature Strengths" is your gift back to God. What are *your* first fruits and are you carrying them well?

Internalize & Actualize:

1. Write a list of your five top strengths. How are you tapping into these strengths in your day-to-day life? What can you be being doing to utilize them more?

   _____

   _____

   _____

2. What are your weaknesses? How can you use the strengths you just listed to help overcome or transform your weaknesses?

   _____

   _____

   _____

3. What are the pitfalls of your strengths? What are you doing to ensure that they remain positive and that you don't cave into their destructive powers? Below, write a thank you letter for these gifts and for the ability to utilize them in the proper way.

   _____

   _____

   _____

THE SEARCH FOR MEANING

(*Nitzavim*/Deuteronomy 29:10 – 30:20)

"If you don't know what you're living for, you haven't yet lived."

- Rabbi Noach Weinberg

There is a familiar story of a man searching the sidewalk for his keys and looking frantically under the streetlight. When questioned by a passerby as to where he may have lost his keys, the man admits that he lost the keys inside his house. Since the light was so much brighter outside under the streetlight, however, he thought it best to look there.

We read this and think what a fool, looking for his lost object in obviously the wrong place, just because it is the "easiest" place to look. But at least this fool knows what he lost and where he lost it. Can we say the same? Many of us are not only looking in the wrong place for our lost objects, but we are even not sure what we're looking for. And yet, we are driven to search on and on. To what end?

According to Freud, the primary drive of man is the pursuit of pleasure. "Not so," said Nietzsche, "the primary drive of man is the pursuit of power." Viktor Frankl, the famous Viennese psychiatrist who suffered for three years in concentration camps during the Holocaust and who endured the murder of his entire family and pregnant wife, nevertheless founded "logo-therapy," which is the theory that the primary drive of man is not pleasure or power, but the search for meaning.

Many of us have an inner ache, a discontented restlessness, without knowing why. Viktor Frankl coined the term, "Sunday Neurosis," an existential anxiety that is formed from the vague awareness people get that their lives are empty and meaningless when they are not otherwise distracted by the work week. Some remained bored and apathetic; others try to fill the void. But it's of no use, because we cannot fill a spiritual hole with non-spiritual stuff. Yet, we keep trying.

Accordingly, if man's primary drive is the search for meaning, where do we look? If it's not in the Himalayas, the ashram, the shrink's couch, the self-help section of the bookstore, the office, the lab, the studio, the field, or even the sanctuary… then where?

In the Torah portion, *"Nitzavim,"* Moses tells us exactly where to look. "It is not in heaven…. Nor is it across the sea…. Rather, the matter is very near to you – in your mouth and your heart - to perform it."[70] Moses spoke these words to the Jewish people on the last day of his life - knowing that it was the last day of his life. The stakes couldn't be higher. What is this matter "that is near and dear that we are to perform"? To love God, to walk in His ways, and to observe His commandments. In a word, to embody the Torah.

Wait - did I just lose you? "Sorry," you say, "but Torah is not the meaning of my life. I'm outta here." If your view of Torah is that it is a bunch of dry, archaic "do's" and "don'ts," commanding strict, automaton-like adherence to meaningless and empty ritual, then I would totally agree with you. I wouldn't find that meaningful in the slightest. But that's not my view of the "matter of Torah."

The Matter of the Matter

I like what Abraham Lincoln had to say about this: "I care not for a man's religion whose dog and cat are not the better for it." And so, if your religion doesn't make you a better person, a better spouse, parent, friend, and lover of your fellow, it's not the "matter of Torah." If your religion doesn't make you compassionate and yearn to alleviate suffering, it's not the "matter of Torah." And if you are not inspired to love justice and truth, striving to live humbly with integrity, then it's simply not the "matter of Torah."

The "matter of Torah" that Moses tells us to look for is within us. It has to be real, and we have to own it. Otherwise, it may as well be high up in the heavens or across the distant sea – it means nothing as it is too far out of our orbit to be relevant. But let's be clear. It is we who push Torah away, and who say it's not relevant or accessible. And as long as we keep this lie on our lips, we will keep looking for meaning under that streetlight and all other extraneous places.

That doesn't mean we get to decide on our own what Torah is or what it means. It doesn't mean that we can overlay the Torah with the imprimatur of our emotions, political viewpoints, etc. Many phenomena exist objectively and independent of us. Certain things just "are," like gravity, which doesn't need our "buy-in" to be real and to affect us. On the other hand, while Torah also has an independent truth and reality, Torah very much wants our "buy-in." God wants our partnership!

And that is the challenge – to take the light of an independent Godly reality, and, through loving God, walking in His ways and observing His commandments, understand that it is *our* reality also. We ask God to "circumcise our hearts," to remove the spiritual impediments and barriers that keeps us locked in the illusion of separation from God – and each other.

Tradition teaches that when we are in the womb, an angel teaches us all of Torah, but that we forget it when we are born. We only "forget" it on the conscious level, however. After birth, the memories of all of our experiences lodge within us on a cellular level and that is why learning Torah is re-discovering Torah, and uncovering a truth we already hold within.

When our hearts beat with the knowledge of this truth within us, then the "matter" is in our mouths. It drives our speech and our actions. It's who we are at our core. When an inauthentic persona does not imprison us, we are free to live in the joyful vibrancy of a congruent life.

While we are necessarily concerned with finding the meaning of our lives, let us start by finding the meaning of life itself. Ultimately, we will find our real purpose and ourselves. Then, the object and the light will coincide, and, unlike the fool, we will be looking for the right thing in the right place, where it always was and where it always will be.

Internalize & Actualize:

1. What are three things you are looking for in your life? Where have you been looking for them? Do you feel you are looking in the right place? If not, where do you feel you need to be looking that you have perhaps been avoiding?

   _____

   _____

   _____

2. We often mistakenly believe that if we have certain external things, that we will be happy, fulfilled, successful, etc. What are those things for you? How do you think they will change things for you and why?

   _____

   _____

   _____

3. Close your eyes, take a deep look within, and focus on all the strengths, abilities, talents and gifts that you have internally. How can you use what you already have and what you already are, to find the other things you are looking for in your life?

   _____

   _____

   _____

DO THE RIGHT THING –
IT'S NOT THAT HARD

(*Vayeilech*/Deuteronomy 31:1 – 30)

"All we can do to prepare rightly for tomorrow is to do the right thing today."

- Wendell Barry

Hey, everyone. It's my birthday today. I'm 120 years old! And today is the last day of my life. Thus, (paraphrasing, of course), begins the Torah portion, "*Vayeilech,*" which chronicles Moses' farewell to the Jewish people, in which he gives his final words of instruction and comfort, and passes on the baton of leadership to Joshua.

Unlike Moses, however, most of us don't know the actual day of our death. Proponents of mindfulness exhort us, however, to imagine that it was, with positive clichés and variations of "*Carpe Diem,*" as if urging us to live each day as if it were our last would somehow cure our existential procrastination. But that doesn't work for me. *Last day, huh? OK, I think I'll have the nachos grande (with sour cream, of course), an order of mozzarella sticks and a pineapple mojito. Veggie burger on a lettuce wrap? Don't think so.* In other words, "*Seize the day!*" doesn't necessarily lead me to the right place.

Living Future Forward

Instead of pretending - (hopefully so) - that today were the *last day* of your life, what if you were to realize, instead, that it's the *first day* of the *rest* of your life? What if you could make use of a preferred future to inspire and focus your present behavior? What if you could hold a vision of a realized potential, and chart a path towards that goal? *How great would it be to age with vitality and quality of life and still show up for Flamenco classes at age 75? Hmm, that veggie burger sounds pretty good after all.*

Getting the Right Advice

I had a client who was struggling with "doing the right thing." Knowing how important this man's relationship was with his son, and how he wanted to be a good role model as a dad, I asked him classic coaching questions: "How would you want your son to toast you at your 80th birthday party? What do you want your son to say about you at your funeral? What is the legacy you want to leave behind?" And if his present behavior were out of alignment with a future that he wished to be true, then he would need to adjust the trajectory of his conduct. Thus, as a technique for shaping present behavior, fast –forwarding twenty, thirty or more years and even to an imagined deathbed, is a powerful exercise.

Another technique is to look at the big picture. When an upset intrudes into my life, for example, I ask myself whether this drama will exist or matter in five years, or ten years, or at the end of my life. Knowing that I probably won't even remember something in the future that's bothering me now, gives me the healthy perspective I need to make better choices about how to cope.

From Your Wiser Future Self

On the other hand, when I am struggling with a decision, I can also ask my future self whether I will someday regret that I didn't make a particular choice. I visualize looking back on my life as having gone down either path, and I imagine how I will feel having lived with the consequences of each choice. Will I feel remorse or peace, sorrow or fulfillment?

What Does Science Say?

Researchers look to science for the keys to "doing the right thing" and have come up with a fascinating experiment testing whether projecting oneself into the future could shape better decisions for today.[71] Groups of college students were asked what they would do if they were strapped financially, needed a new computer, and were told by a friend that he happened to know where they could get one cheap – wink-wink, nod-nod.

Before answering that question, however, all of the students were directed to write a letter to their future selves – describing themselves as if the future were now. One group was told to write to a future self three months hence, and the other group was told to write a letter to a future self twenty years out. And then they answered the question whether they would buy a stolen computer or not.

The students who wrote letters to themselves in the near future were much more likely to take the offer while those who wrote to a distant future self were much more apt to decline it. The reason is simple. Imagining yourself three months from now doesn't give you a different perspective. You're still in your same skin, identified with the "now" of your life. So, if your present self were tempted by the offer, projecting three months into the future would be irrelevant.

When students described their imagined self in twenty years, however, they were able to step out of their narrative and craft a preferred vision of themselves. And as if this wiser and future doppelganger were reaching back in time, these students tended to make better choices that aligned with that wiser and better self.

Take the Moses Challenge

Try writing your obituary. Who will you be at the end of your days? What will have mattered and what won't? What do you want your loved ones to say about you – and to have learned from you? What do you want to leave as your legacy? And then work your way backward – to today – and make choices that are designed to get you there. Says one who is wise beyond his years, the famous Puss 'n Boots, "It's never too late to do the right thing." You're always one decision away from a totally different life. Do one thing today your future self will thank you for - it's easier than you think.

Internalize & Actualize:

1. When you were asked to write your obituary, how did that make you feel? No one wants to think about his or her death, but what was the initial response or feeling that you had? Use that feeling to motivate how you now think about your future. If you responded with dread that you haven't done what you want to do, write down five things you can start doing to change that. If you felt at peace that you have lived a productive, fulfilled life, write down what led to that and how you can continue to increase what you are doing for even more satisfaction.

   _____

   _____

   _____

2. Think about a mistake you have made that at the time felt irreparable. Looking back now, was it as damaging as you initially thought? Even if the consequences were grave, what have you have learned from that and how has it shaped you?

   _____

   _____

   _____

3. What is something you are worried about now? Is it something fixable? Will it be something that stays with you in the future? Write about this situation but in ten years and see how much of an impact it will really have and use that to help determine how much of your time and energy should be focused on it at this point in your life.

   _____

   _____

   _____

53

FINDING OUR SONG

(*Ha'azinu*/Deuteronomy 32:1 – 52)

"The search for meaning is really the search for the lost chord. When the lost chord is discovered by humankind, the discord in the world will be healed and the symphony of the universe will come into complete harmony with itself."

- John O'Donohue

The Happiest Place on Earth

For our 20th wedding anniversary, we decided to make a dream come true – a trip to Disney World - without the kids. As we entered the parking lot of the resort, the attendant at the gate warmly said to us, "Welcome home." *Wow, that's so nice*, I thought, impressed with Disney's hospitality training.

As the car ride to Orlando was a long one, by the time we arrived, the floor of the front seat was strewn with empty coffee cups and wrappers from bags of chips and organic coconut cookies. Having no plastic bag, I clumped the trash into my hands and headed for the hotel assuming there would be a trashcan outside of the lobby entrance. Alas, there wasn't. But as I walked into the elegant lobby, awkwardly clutching my garbage, the hotel greeter (who was dressed like a guard from Buckingham Palace) held out his big hands and said, "Here, let me take that." I was mortified and refused the offer, preferring instead just to be directed to a trashcan. "No need for that," he replied with a smile, "After all, you're home now."

I looked carefully into his eyes to determine if the smile was genuine. According to French neurologist Guillaume Duchenne, authentic smiles based on positive emotion involuntarily engage the muscles around the eyes, as opposed to fake smiles in which only the mouth moves. There it was – a genuine Duchenne smile. Realizing he was *sincerely* happy to be handed my garbage, I weakly raised up my hands, loosened my grasp and let go.

I liked this new "home" I found myself in. After all, no one cheerfully asked to throw out my trash in any home in which I ever lived. As I looked around the well-appointed lobby of my "new home," I noticed the flowers, the music, and everyone moving about with happiness and delight. Compared to what I was used to, it was so perfect. *Maybe I'm dead*, I wondered. *Maybe my husband and I died instantly in a car crash on the way to Orlando, and now we're in heaven. Could be worse.* Just then, I saw a frustrated mother dragging a crying, balking child by the hand. *Oh good, I'm not dead*, I realized, as reality checked in.

The Song of the Soul

Life, as we all know, it not a Disney movie, and home is not a Disney resort. With all of its suffering, stresses, and tests, however, real life is still one heckuva ride. In the Torah portion of *Ha'azinu*, which is referred to as Moses' farewell song to the Jewish people, Moses recaps the good, the bad and the ugly. Neither holding back criticism of past behavior nor mincing words about the dire future consequences of bad choices, Moses nevertheless inspires the people with a vision of ultimate victory and final redemption. No matter the trials and tribulations the Jewish people endured – and will endure – the deep connection between God and the Jewish people is an everlastingly unbreakable and unshakable bond.

Sympathetic Vibration

So, what is a "song?" Says Rabbi Gedalia Schorr in a publication called *Torah Weekly,* a song is a sympathetic vibration. "Just as all the notes in a chord and all the voices and instruments in an orchestra blend together to form a single sound, so all creation *sings* in harmony to proclaim Hashem's (God's) Unity."[72] That *Ha'azinu* is written in the form of a song, so are we to understand that whether for good or bad, all of creation resonates in harmony.

Thus, our imperfections form part of a perfect destiny - driven whole. In fact, the very heaven and earth that God created in the opening verse of the Torah — those eternal sentinels - are now beckoned to hear and witness Moses' song in which past present and future combine in a timeless coherence. Although *Ha'azinu* is the next to the last chapter of the Torah, we read it on the first Shabbat following Rosh Hashanah (the New Year). As endings merge with new beginnings, Moses dies, and Adam is born.

Our Heart Song

Occurring between Rosh Hashanah and Yom Kippur, *Ha'azinu* falls on one of the holiest Sabbaths of the year, where we engage in deep introspection and reset our intentions for the coming year. *Ha'azinu,* however, reminds us we were imperfect in the past, and despite our best intentions, we will be so in the future. But just as God doesn't expect perfection from us; neither should we expect God to grant us Disney perfect lives. While it may sound discordant at times, we each have a song to sing and a voice to be heard. Inner harmony is not about perfection; rather it's about connection. The music we make becomes the songs of our lives, blending into the vast timeless symphony of Creation, which, nevertheless, connects us to God and each other. *It's a small world, after all.*

Internalize and Actualize:

1. Where do you feel most at home? And do you feel at home within yourself? Do others feel at home when they are with you? Now write down the qualities that define "home" for you. Are all of these healthy qualities? Are there any you want to work on or add?

   _____

   _____

   _____

2. Think about where you were at this time last year. How have you grown and developed in this year? What has changed about you? Write down five positive things that have happened that could not have happened a year ago. Then write down five areas you would like to work on. Think about yourself a year from now, how do you want those five things to be different? What can you start doing now to ensure they will be?

   _____

   _____

   _____

3. You have a song, a unique song that was written and continues to be written and sung just by you and for you. How do you want your song to sound? What do you want it to say? Think about the voices and instruments you want representing it. Then try to listen to it in your head. How does it make you feel? Can you sing your song?

   _____

   _____

   _____

A WHOLE-HEARTED AFFAIR

(*Vzot Haberachah*/Deuteronomy 33:1 – 34:12)

*"At a certain point, you have to kind of realize
that greatness is a messy thing."*

- James Gray

Contrary to popular belief, people with OCD are not necessarily neat freaks. Case in point: I can function perfectly well in a messy and disorganized kitchen; however, I don't like to put away leftover food (such as a pan of lasagna) with a ragged untidy end. Therefore, I will carefully cut off the uneven bit, justify to myself the moral imperative of eating it and then sigh with satisfaction at the resulting perfectly straight 90° edge. Whether it's OCD or a vestige from my woodworking days, I have a strong preference for objects to be level, centered, and squared-off with straight lines. I also like bucket seats, edged flower borders and TV dinners from the 70's that separate food into little compartments.

And so, the cycle of reading the Torah seems rather messy to me, in that it doesn't end nice and neat with Rosh Hashanah (the Jewish New Year). As a matter of fact, several Torah portions spill over into the next year, and *Vzot Haberachah,* which is the last portion of the Torah, comes at the very tail end of the Jewish holidays (Simchat Torah). Furthermore, as it is the only Torah portion not read in synagogue on a Sabbath, I strongly considered not even including in this book, but then there would have been 53 chapters – not 54 - and I prefer even numbers.

Happy New Year – Now Fix Yourself

In the secular calendar, January 1ˢᵗ is synonymous with making New Year's resolutions. That is why gyms and organization such as Weight Watchers, offer special incentives to join at this time of the year when motivation, as well as false hopes, ride exceptionally high. Statistically, 80% of such resolutions fail by the second week of February, and overall, studies suggest that far less than 10% of us achieve our resolution goals.

One study I saw on New Year's statistics broke down success in achieving goals within age groups, and the least successful was the over-fifty set.[73] That came as a surprise to me since the ever-increasing awareness of my mortality is a powerful incentive to consider Hillel's famous question, "If not now, when?" But then I thought of the damage that can occur to psyches that have experienced repeated cycles of failure over decades. Eventually, people either don't even try anymore or make half-hearted attempts with guaranteed disappointment waiting to happen, which then reinforces a fixed view of themselves – and the universe - in which they come up short.

It's All about Love

The secular New Year's resolutions center around weighing less, earning more, getting in shape, getting organized and kicking an addiction. In contrast, the themes of the Jewish holidays (Rosh Hashanah, Yom Kippur, Sukkot and Simchat Torah) are about *relationships* – coming closer and connecting to God, repairing our relationships with other people, and ultimately engaging in honest self-discovery to make conscious choices for personal growth.

Thus, the Torah doesn't end all nice and neat and tidy way at the end of the Jewish year, because life and learning are messy affairs without straight lines and clean edges. Furthermore, as soon as we read the last sentence of the last verse of the Torah, with our very next breath we begin the reading of the Torah all over again - because the growth process is never ending.

In words that resonate with modern ears, Aristotle famously said, "We are what we repeatedly do. Greatness then is not an act, but a habit." In short, we are what we practice. For example, if you consistently engage in an unwanted behavior, over time you will have had a lot of practice at it, and by now, you are probably very good at being the very thing you least desire.

Granted, it is far from easy, but when you change what you are doing, you can change whom you are being. And so, while practice makes perfect, practice itself is never perfect – hence the term. It's all about making mistakes and learning from them and recommitting over and over to a goal. One day at a time.

Healthy Resolutions

When we come to the end of the Torah, we should be looking back at how we have lived the prior year, while at the same time, as we begin the cycle anew, we can reflect upon how to practice better in the coming year. Thus, the "failures" we will undoubtedly experience can be redefined from being a setback that reinforces a negative self-image that cannot be changed, to a valuable opportunity for learning and growth on the path of fulfilling potential. This approach requires compassion for others as well as for oneself.

To that end, the last letter of the Torah is a *lamed* (pronounced "l"). And the first letter of the Torah is a *beit* (pronounced "v"). Together, these two letters from the word *"lev,"* which means "heart." Thus, Torah is not merely a cerebral mind game but a full-fledged heart game, because spiritual growth is a whole-hearted affair. And we are never alone in that process.

In *Vzot Haberachah*, Moses blesses each of the tribes with its unique strengths and gifts. We should understand that each of us contains the spiritual DNA - not just of the patriarchs and matriarchs - but of all the tribes as well. Just as no two people have the same genetic code (not even identical twins, as it turns out), we are all blessed with these multiple attributes to the extent that we need them for our unique spiritual mission.

Thus, as we go through our tests and challenges, we are never without the resources, tools and inner strength we need to turn crisis into opportunity and suffering into growth. While we all may want to live by design, lives of inspiration are nevertheless messy, and therefore, our reasonable goal should not be unattainable perfection but an ever-present desire to grow and connect.

Nadine Stair, an eighty-five-year-old from Louisville, Kentucky said, "Oh, I've had my moments, and if I had to do it over again, I'd have more of them. I'd try to have nothing else."[74] So, here is to your 'what was' and what will be *your* year of sacred moments, your journey of spiritual growth and heart-based Torah, and may you fill your endings with many new beginnings.

Internalize and Actualize:

1. Write down a few resolutions or promises that you made that repeatedly get broken. How do you feel about these things when you think about them? Now, write next to those resolutions something practical you can do in each area, starting *today*, that will work towards those end goals. Make sure it is something small so that you can stick to it.

   _____

   _____

   _____

2. Now write down some commitments you are able to make in the following areas: Friends, Family, Yourself, Spirituality. In each area, write down something practical that you can do to further connect to those you love, to yourself and your needs and to your Creator. Again, this should be something doable that you can implement into your life.

   _____

   _____

   _____

3. If you have gone through this entire book, you have spent significant time thinking about yourself, your purpose, your goals and your future. Mazal Tov! That is quite an accomplishment to have put that much focus into such things. Now, as this book concludes - only to begin anew - write down five of the most significant things you have learned about yourself through this process. And make sure to date it, as when you reach this point the next time, you will want to compare where you are now to where you will be then!

_____

_____

_____

END NOTES

1   John Gottman, *The Seven Principles for Making Marriage Work* (New York: Harmony Books, 2015 2nd ed.), pps. 36-38. See also <u>The Four Horsemen - The Gottman Institute.</u> https://www.gottman.com › The Gottman Relationship Blog.

2   Rabbi Schneur Zalman of Liadi (Russia 1745-1812). Rabbi Schneur Zalman, the founder of Chabad Chassidism, drew from all previous mystical and Talmudic teachings to create the most comprehensive blueprint for modern life, uniting faith and reason, spirit and matter. https://www.meaningfullife.com/alter-rebbe/.

3   Viktor Frankl, *Man's Search for Meaning* (New York: Washington Square Press 1959 updated and revised edition). Originally published in Austria in 1946.

4   http://alifeoflight.com/daily-inspirational-messages/ "At ALifeofLight, our mission is simple; we help people around the world change their lives for the better. So every day they can be happier, more positive, more abundant, more awesome."

5   Brené Brown, *The Gifts of Imperfection: Let Go of Who You're Supposed to Be and Embrace Who You Are* (Center City, Minnesota: Hazeldon 2010).

6   https://lyndawallace.com/.

7   *Bereishit*/Genesis 12:1.

8   http://rabbilevitt.blogspot.com/2012/10/parshat-lech-lecha.html.

9   The Meshech Chochmah (Rabbi Meir Simcha of Dvinsk 1843 – 1926) the Meshech Chochma reads the first verse of *Lech Lecha* in the following way: "Go forth from your land....to the place where I will show YOU to yourself." Says Rabbi Alex Israel: "According to this understanding, this journey is not simply a geographical relocation, it is a personal transformation. In the promised land Avraham will find himself. He will realise his true potential. This will not be to Avraham's benefit alone. God will also 'show' him to the world, indicating to others the dedication to God that is a possibility for all individuals." http://www.alexisrael.org/lech-lecha---abrahams-journey.

10 Shefali Tsabary, *The Conscious Parent: Transforming Ourselves and Empowering Our Children* (Vancouver, Canada: Namaste Publishing 2010).

11 *Bereishit*/Genesis 23:1.

12 Susan Cain, *Quiet: The Power of an Introvert in a World That Can't Stop Talking* (New York: Random House 2012).

13 *Bereishit*/Genesis 25:19.

14 https://www.alephbeta.org/course/lecture/toldot-what-is-isaa.

15 Kristin Neff, *Self-Compassion: Stop Beating Yourself Up and Leave Insecurity Behind* (Harper Collins e-books) pps. 65-66.

16 Harville Hendrix, Helen LaKelly Hunt, *Receiving Love: Letting Yourself be Transformed by Letting Yourself Be Loved* (New York: Atria Books 2004).

17 Viktor Frankl, *Man's Search for Meaning* (New York: Washington Square Press 1959 updated and revised edition). Originally published in Austria in 1946.

18 Neil Soggie, *Logotherapy: Viktor Frankl, His Life and Work* (Lanam, Maryland: Roman and Littlefield 2016).

19 *Bereishit*/Genesis 42:8.

20 https://www.forbes.com/sites/hbsworkingknowledge/2016/05/18/unethical-amnesia-whey-we-tend-to-forget-our-own-bad-behavior/#5c79ddbf766c.

21 Based on a talk, "Honest Liars -- the Psychology of Self-deception: Cortney Warren at TEDxUNLV: https://www.youtube.com/watch?v=YpEeSa6zBTE.

22 http://www.everydaypsychology.com/2007/04/sense-of-coherence.html#. WQ-Tw8m1smI.

23 Lisa Cron, *Wired for Story: The Writer's Guide to Using Brain Science to Hook Readers from the Very First Sentence* (New York: Ten Speed Press, 2012).

24 See for example, David Cooperider, Diana Whitney, *Appreciative Inquiry: A Positive Revolution in Change* (San Francisco, California: Berrett-Koehler Publishers, Inc. 2005).

25 *Vayeishev*/Genesis 37:1.

26 "Do not be distressed, nor reproach yourselves for having sold me here, for it was to be a provider that God sent me ahead of you....And now, it was not you who sent me here, but God." Vayigash/Genesis 45:4-8.

27 Danny Inny. https://mail.google.com/mail/u/0/#inbox/15be339038601817. https://mirasee.com/about-us/danny-iny/.

28 *Shemot*/Exodus 3:2-5.

29 Parker Palmer, *The Courage to Teach* (San Francisco, California: John Wiley & Sons 2007 Tenth Anniversary Edition) p. 65.

30 Ecclesiastes 3:1.

31 There are six things that the Torah commands us to remember. Optimally, these verses should be recited out loud each day and their meanings should be considered. https://www.ou.org/torah/mitzvot/taryag/the_six_remembrances/.

32 *Devarim*/Deuteronomy 16:3.

33 Cooperider and Whitney (2005).

34 *Shemot*/Exodus 12:2.

[35] In Rabbi David Aaron's book, *The God-Powered Life: Awakening to Your True Purpose* (Boston and London: Trumpeter 2012), pps. 40-43, Rabbi Aaron discusses the dual nature of man, divided between his creative energies and spiritual longings, as derived from the work of Joseph B. Soloveitchik, *The Lonely Man of Faith* (New York: Doubleday 1965).

[36] Jim Collins, Jerry Porras, *Built to Last: Successful Habits of Visionary Companies* (New York: Harper Business 1994).

[37] Isaiah 30:26.

[38] Aaron, at p. 42.

[39] Shawn Achor, *Before Happiness* (New York: Crown Business 2013) pps. 12-13.

[40] Martin Seligman, *Learned Optimism*: *How to Change Your Mind and Your Life* (New York: Vintage Books, 2nd ed. 2006). See pps. 3-5.

[41] Kristin Neff, *Self-Compassion: Stop Beating Yourself Up and Leave Insecurity Behind* (Harper Collins e-books) pps. 8-10.

[42] Lalin Anik, Lara Aknin, Michael Norton, Elizabeth Dunn, published a working paper for the Harvard Business School, *Feeling Good About Giving: The Benefits (and Costs) of Self Interested Charitable Behavior* (2010). http://www.hbs.edu/faculty/Publication%20Files/10-012.pdf.

[43] http://www.mesora.org/RabbiFox/Tetzaveh65.htm.

[44] Daryl Bem, *Self Perception Theory* (published in Advances in Experimental Social Psychology vol. 6 1972) http://www.dbem.us/SP%20Theory.pdf.

[45] Saul McCloud, The Milgram Experiment (published in Simply Psychology 2007), https://www.simplypsychology.org/milgram.html.

[46] *Shemot*/Exodus 25:8.

[47] Rabbi Yissachar Frand, Hearing Voices from Heaven June 7, 2007 http://torah.org/torah-portion/ravfrand-5760-vayikra/.

[48] Achor, at page 153.

[49] *Id*. At 149.

[50] Rabbi Shneur, The Pursuit of the Spiritual Life, April 2016. https://thearkcentre.org.au/april-2016-parshat-shemini-the-pursuit-of-the-spiritual-life/.

[51] *Vayikra*/Leviticus (10:3).

[52] Bureau of Justice Statistics https://www.bjs.gov/index.cfm?ty=tp&tid=17.

[53] Based on Sichas Shabbos Parshas Emor, 5750. http://www.congregationlubavitch.org/page.asp?pageID=%7B67BD59F8-7DBA-4A5C-AEB7-46CDF1DB90D4%7D.

[54] Brené Brown, The Power of Vulnerability (Ted Talk June 2010). https://www.ted.com/talks/brene_brown_on_vulnerability.

[55] *See* Jim Collins, Jerry Porras J, *Built to Last: Successful Habits of Visionary Companies* (New York: Harper Business 1994).

[56] *Bamidbar*/Numbers 4:1-9.

57 The Losada Ratio is the sum of the positivity in a system divided by the sum of its negativity. A ratio of 3.0 to 6.0 has been found to be highly correlated with high performance. "The Power of Positivity, In Moderation: The Losada Ratio," http://happierhuman.com/losada-ratio/.

58 "The Positive Perspective: Dr. Gottman's Magic Ratio," https://www.gottman.com/blog/the-positive-perspective-dr-gottmans-magic-ratio/.

59 This quote is attributed to several people.

60 *Bamidbar*/Numbers 16:3.

61 *Bamidbar*/Numbers 24:5.

62 https://www.thenation.com/article/optimism-uncertainty/.

63 *Devarim*/Deuteronomy 1:27.

64 https://www.washingtonpost.com/lifestyle/magazine/pearls-before-breakfast-can-one-of-the-nations-great-musicians-cut-through-the-fog-of-a-dc-rush-hour-lets-find-out/2014/09/23/8a6d46da-4331-11e4-b47c-f5889e061e5f_story.html?utm_term=.6a211afe30dd.

65 *Devarim*/Deuteronomy 11:26.

66 *Devarim*/Deuteronomy 12:28.

67 Quote attributed to Henry Ford.

68 *Devarim*/Deuteronomy 8:8.

69 https://www.authentichappiness.sas.upenn.edu/.

70 *Devarim*/Deuteronomy 30:11-14.

71 https://insight.kellogg.northwestern.edu/article/for_long_range_thinking_imagine_the_future_self.

72 https://ohr.edu/tw/5757/devarim/haazinu.htm.

73 http://www.statisticbrain.com/new-years-resolution-statistics/.

74 As quoted by Jon Kabat-Zinn, *Full Catastrophe Living* (New York: Dell Publishing 1990) p.17.

NOTES

NOTES

NOTES

NOTES

NOTES

NOTES

NOTES

NOTES

NOTES

NOTES

Printed in the United States
By Bookmasters